Lettice Curtis

Her Autobiography

First hardback edition published in 2004.
This softback second edition published by;

Red Kite
PO Box 223
Walton on Thames
Surrey
KT12 3YQ
England
Tel. 0845 095 0346

www.redkitebooks.co.uk

Designed by Mark Postlethwaite
Printed and bound in the UK by 4edge Limited, Essex.

ISBN 978-1-906592-14-1

Purchase this and other Red Kite books from our online store;

www.wingleader.co.uk

Lettice Curtis

Her Autobiography

Contents

FOREWORD

Inevitably as I write, my thoughts go back to one-time close friends who have changed the course of my life, but are no longer with us.

Frankie Francis, the Commanding Officer of No.1 ATA Ferry Pool allowed me to join his all male ferry pool at White Waltham, and put me forward as the first female for four-engine training. My years in No.1 Pool where many of my fellow pilots became very good friends, were amongst the happiest of my life.

Group Captain Bruin Purvis, Commanding Officer of the Civil Aircraft Test Section at Boscombe Down, who was prepared to take me on as one of his test pilots, but was stopped from so doing by high-ups in the Ministry. After accepting a job instead in the Performance Division of the A&AEE and attached to his section, I spent happy years there as a flight test observer, during which Bruin changed from being just the boss, to another very good friend. As did his second in command, test pilot 'Doc' Stuart, with whom I also shared many happy times both whilst I was at Boscombe and after I left. We still met often until, in 1986, I visited him in St Stephens hospital, which was where he died.

I met Joan Hughes who comes into the ATA story, when we were both in the women's ferry pool at Hatfield and after ATA, living nearby, we kept in close touch until in 1993 she too died. Had she been around when I was preparing this book, her help would have been invaluable for checking on memories of our ATA friends and on our ATA lives.

Lastly not to be forgotten is John Hassell, Joint Managing Director of G.T.Foulis & Co, who when turned down by other aviation publishers, took on in 1971 the publication of my first book 'The Forgotten Pilots', a history of the Air Transport Auxiliary. I remember him telling me in those computer-less days, that no less that five hand-typed drafts were prepared.

Through my job at Boscombe, although it was a minor one, I met and came to know many test pilots, both civil and military, a number of whom I am happy to say at the time of writing, I still meet at various aviation functions. Over the years I have been accepted into a number of aviation societies, more on account of my writing than through my flying, which in later years became singularly unspectacular when they became simply a matter of doing enough light-aircraft flying to keep up my license.

Lettice Curtis 2004

CHAPTER 1

DENBURY

Prior to WW1 my parents had moved to Denbury Manor in the small Devon village of Denbury, some four miles south-west of Newton Abbot, where at the time many villagers were born, lived and died without contact with the outside world. It was the late twenties before electricity arrived and I still have vivid memories of the row of oil lamps lined up each morning in the pantry to be cleaned. We went to bed by candle-light. Later 'Aladdins', a new type of oil lamp with a mantle, became fashionable and were used downstairs. These gave a better light but had a habit, if left on their own, of 'smoking' and more often than not we would return to the drawing room after dinner to find the atmosphere thick and the furniture covered with oily smuts; in days before vacuum cleaners this led to a great deal of cleaning.

The telephone arrived when six people in the village could be found to subscribe. As well as ourselves the six I recall included the village butcher and the rector. Our number was Ipplepen 6 and you had to count the number of rings to know if the call was for you. If you picked up the phone when it was not for you, you could listen to others conversing!

There was great excitement when a morning and evening bus started running from the village to Newton Abbot. We had at the time a 'Mademoiselle' and previous to its arrival she walked the four miles each way to attend her Roman Catholic church in Newton Abbot.

My older sister, Gabrielle, was first taught at home by 'Mademoiselle' the governess, and went on to St. James, in West Malvern, an up-market school where education revolved around their pupils' social skills and no exams were taken. With a large family, however, my father had, by the 1920s, said that in the post-war world girls as well as boys would have to earn their living and to this end should be given a similar education. At that time this was remarkable forward thinking and certainly something for which I have been ever grateful.

Denbury Manor

By the time I was six there were already two younger ones in the family and another one on the way; this meant retaining the full-time nurse who had been taken on for me – and who ever afterwards referred to me as 'her first baby.' With all attention now going to the younger ones I was sent away as a weekly boarder to Cumberland House, a school in nearby Paignton. Here the only other boarder was a boy of similar age called Monty. Monty and I therefore shared everything including, as far as I remember, a bedroom. Whilst there we both caught whooping cough and were sent to a farm at Rickham, near Salcombe, to recuperate; here we ran wild and thoroughly enjoyed ourselves.

At home one day, whilst Nurse was bathing my brother, I was relating incidents from life at Paignton and how Monty and I did everything together including sharing a bath. This information horrified Nurse, who said so in no mean terms and reported the matter to my mother. The next thing I knew was that I had been taken away from Cumberland House and sent as a full-time boarder to St. Catherine's School in Bude, a girls' school on the north coast of Cornwall; it was there that I celebrated my seventh birthday. Living as we did in the depths of the country, there can have been no alternative to boarding, as, in the days before regular bus services, arranging transport to a day school in Newton Abbot some four miles away would have caused insoluble problems. In fact, a few years later my younger brother and sister were sent for their early education to a school in Newton Abbot, taken there in the pony and trap.

In the early twenties my father acquired two cars, one for himself and one for my mother; both were Buicks. My father's was a grey two-seater with, in place of a rear seat, a 'dicky' (described in my dictionary as a folding seat at the back of a vehicle), which consisted of a large panel which when raised exposed a double bench seat. There was no head cover for this seat, but nevertheless it was one we fought to sit in. My mother's car was a dark blue tourer with wide bench seats front and back and in place of fixed windows, flexible side-screens that could be removed in fine weather. This was intended for my mother to use for shopping in Newton Abbot and to transport the children about; it was the car in which, many years later, I learned to drive. The cars were inevitably referred to as the 'grey car' and the 'blue car', and the first we learned about their arrival was when we found that the Brougham and pony trap had been replaced in the coach house by the cars.

With the arrival of his car, my father stepped up his visits to the Royal Southern Yacht Club in Torquay, whither he had previously gone in the pony and trap. For this he had wrapped himself in a heavy tweed overcoat and put a rug of many colours (which we called 'Jacob's coat') over his knees. Thus attired he would drive to his club in all weathers, taking sandwiches in a silver sandwich box engraved with his monogram. To tell the time he had a carriage clock which was passed on to me when I went to Oxford and is still one of my treasured possessions.

A full time boarder in Bude at the age of seven!

At the club my father would read any newspapers he had not seen read at home, where we took The Times, The Morning Post and a number of picture papers. He also played billiards, at which he became an accomplished player. Sometimes we would go with him to Torquay and, whilst he was in the club, go to the cinema or bathe from Meadfoot beach or in the seawater baths near where the car was parked. We were told to be back in the car by six o'clock, but well before this we were usually ready to go home. We often had a long wait, especially if my father was playing billiards, when he might not appear until seven o'clock or even later. Occasionally our mother took us to Torquay in the blue car to visit the dentist or to buy us new clothes for school from Bobby's. On rare occasions we were taken to a show at The Pavilion, after which we would have cream cakes and ices at Addison's.

Dinner at home was served at eight o'clock. I would have been 12 or 13 before I was allowed to take part in it, and I had to wear a dress. For dinner my father would wear a faded dinner-jacket and a pair of exceedingly ancient patent leather shoes which, when we giggled at them, he would proudly announce were the ones in which he had been married. He took good care of his slim figure, which did not change with age. He took little part in the upbringing of his children which was left to Mother. At home he spent most of his time in his library where he spent many hours reading books and studying family documents. After dinner he would join us in the drawing room where sometimes we played chess, but more often he would sit reading The Times. Part of his remoteness was due to the fact that he was very deaf – the result, I always understood, of measles caught when he was grown up. This had forced him to give up his practice as a barrister for, in those days, the only aid to hearing was an ear-trumpet. By the late twenties, however, he had acquired an Amplivox, a device with an earpiece that he held to his ear while he fiddled with the controls of a microphone which was built into the box.

CHAPTER 2

BUDE

Bude, on the other side of Dartmoor, was for those days a long drive from our home in Denbury near the South Coast and, in any case, the car did not lend itself to transporting the heavy trunks into which clothes and other school impedimenta were in those days packed. When returning to school, therefore, my mother would take me by train to Exeter, where we would have lunch. Afterwards we would join other children also en-route to Bude on the Southern Railways station from where the now long-extinct line ran through Crediton, Okehampton and Holdsworthy to Bude.

St Catherine's was run by three unmarried ladies, no doubt a fall out from the large number of males killed in World War One. Miss Weir was the headmistress, Miss Player was responsible for physical activities and also taught the piano, and Miss Weir's sister Miss Flossie looked after the domestic side of things. It was run by rules laid down by the Parents' National Educational Union (PNEU), a much-used system at the time, the syllabus and no doubt the general lines on which the school was run being dictated by PNEU. This was a first-class education system which gave children a grounding in a wide variety of subjects, many unheard of in prep schools today. I have always felt that I learnt more there than later at my public school where, even then, exams took priority over general knowledge. For instance, as well as piano lessons we were taught the theory of music and how to write it. Painting lessons were part of the normal programme and each term, in a lesson called 'picture study', we were issued with prints of six pictures by famous artists for analysis and discussion. There was also a large library from which I drew heavily until I left at the age of twelve, on Rider Haggard, Dornford Yates and such classics as Lorna Doone and, for some reason, Pilgrims' Progress which I read several times. Books by Scott, Mrs Gaskell and the like were given us for holiday reading, but left little impression on me, and Dickens passed me by. I had piano lessons which I enjoyed and, for a short time at the insistence of my mother, violin lessons which I hated. The school took girls of all ages and I recall no age barriers to our activities although there must have been some, I imagine, in the classroom. At games we all mixed in. We shared dormitories, however, with girls of similar age. The school itself in Downs View consisted of three terraced houses knocked into one. At the back there was an enclosed tarmac playground where we were allowed to roller-skate. At the end of the playground there was a substantial brick building with a roof and three sides where in summer we sometimes had lessons. We were there one day when a distracting sound made the rest of the class look up and I remember being complimented for being the only one to carry on without looking up. I probably reckoned I knew where the sound came from and didn't need to look!

Outside the playground there was an area of grass where in summer we played rounders and cricket, and in winter netball. Cricket bored me as I resented sitting watching others batting. Then there was the beach. For me the main attraction of Bude was the sea and bathing, and I came to love the north Cornish coast in all its weathers. I never remember the sea being completely calm. There were usually breakers and there were strong undercurrents to contend with when bathing as the waves receded. To me the sea was always exciting and a challenge. On summer weekends we took picnics to the beach, lighting fires to boil a kettle; there was always plenty of bread and butter and jam sandwiches to go with it. There was every sort of beach within easy walking distance. Crooklets, a good bathing beach, was within a few hundred yards of the school. There were stony beaches, sandy beaches, beaches enclosed by high cliffs and ones with rock pools containing crabs, small fish and sea anemones which we would never tire of feeding.

Summerleas, Bude's main beach, was all sand. On the south side of it there was a substantial breakwater with a swimming pool called the Pit. At high tide the sea came right over the breakwater so the Pit could only be used when the tide was out. It was in the Pit that I learnt to swim. To reach the breakwater from the beach, water streaming from the canal to the sea had to be crossed. At low tide this was quite shallow and no problem but as the tide came in, the water got ever deeper. I remember an occasion when with the tide coming in we had stayed too long at the Pit, and we waded across the water holding our clothes over our heads.

In winter, except on Sundays when we went to church at Stratton, we went for walks which were for the most part confined to the Downs and to me this was never boring. I liked looking down from the cliffs, watching the waves break on the rocks below and feeling the wind. After a stormy night we would scour the beaches looking for storm wreckage and occasionally we might even sight a wreck. In those days there was no going home at half term and it was rare even for parents to visit. To celebrate a holiday, therefore, special outings would be organised. Places visited included Boscastle, Tintagel and Clovelly, as a special treat we would walk to Coombe some four miles up the coast where we would get a Devonshire Cream tea. As a matter of pride older ones would walk both ways, but for the younger ones there would be a car for the return journey. To celebrate one of my later birthdays I was taken for the first time ever to the cinema, to see The Ten Commandments. Although I have no recollection of what it was about I remember that I was entranced with it. Later, probably on another birthday, I was taken to see The Thief of Baghdad.

It was at Bude that I was introduced to tennis, which remained a life-time interest. When in the spring term it was announced that a coach would be available once a week during the summer for tennis lessons on a pair of grass public courts on the Downs, I immediately wrote home for permission to put my name down. To me it was a chance of a break from cricket. Tennis lessons obviously called for ownership of a tennis racket so my mother rifled the attic and gave me a strange-shaped pre-World War One tennis racket with which I started.

Shortly after arriving at Bude I caught first mumps and then measles. As these diseases were commonplace in those days this was considered a 'good thing' as it meant that you would be unlikely to catch it again in the next school epidemic. I seem to remember that both of these complaints called in those days for three weeks' quarantine. To get over the measles I was sent to a local isolation hospital where one was kept in a dim light to prevent possible eye damage. Sometime later I developed ringworm, caught during the holidays from an older sister's pet rabbits. I only had one spot but at school this was taken very seriously and, without being told why, I was put in a bedroom on my own. My mother told me later that the pillowcases used on my bed were burnt. At home my younger brother and sister, then aged around five and seven, also caught it and, unable to go to school, ran wild for the necessary incubation period.

Although it meant nothing to us at the time, St Catherine's must have had an excellent reputation, as some of the other pupils came from quite a distance. My contemporaries included Margaret, and her younger sister Virginia, Heaton, who in 1942 became the second wife of the Marquis of Northampton. We had to be especially nice to Margaret because she had just lost her mother. Another quiet and often tearful pupil was Gabrielle, later Lady Gabrielle, Courtney - sister of the Earl of Devon, whose father was vicar in Crediton. There were also four Luxmores of which Helen, the second oldest, was my contemporary. She told us that their brother, possibly the only boy in the family, had been killed when he flew into a haystack; my first contact with aviation. My best friend, certainly in later years, was however Barbie Nelson who went on to Wycombe Abbey. I also kept in touch for quite a time with Kitty Simpson who came from Spreyton.

Although there were a few who finished their education at St. Catherine's, most of us moved on at around twelve years of age and I moved to a large and very different school, Benenden. Before I left, my sister Esme (three years younger than me) had joined me at Bude. This was her first time at boarding school and, being unhappy there, she was taken away when I left and sent to a school in Torquay which was nearer home.

CHAPTER 3

BENENDEN

Benenden School came into being in 1923, its co-founders being Christine Sheldon, Anne Hindle and Kathleen Bird. All three were at the time teaching at Wycombe Abbey, but in July 1922 they tendered their resignations and sent out a letter to those they hoped would sponsor them with their proposals for a new girls' public school. Their reasons for founding a new school included a pressing increase in demand for girls' education and a growing reaction against the restrictive discipline in many of the girls' schools and their narrow academic outlook. The new school they planned would provide for girls a broad general education together with a curriculum which would enable them to qualify for a career, and at the same time – as The Times reported – "stimulate in them interests which will enable them to live a full and useful life at home."

Benenden School

Responses to their circular were for the most part from prominent women in girls' schools, colleges at Oxford, Cambridge and
London, and men and women with family connections. They came in
slowly but when they had received some 57 replies the first Council for
the prospective school was called, followed in July 1923 by a formal
announcement of the opening of the new school. The school opened at
Bickley in Kent, leaving the founders with their first job of finding a
permanent home for it.

When Lord Rothermere's home near Cranbrook, Hemsted
Place, came on the market with 300 acres of land at £35,000, they signed
on for a lease of it on Christmas Eve 1924. 'Pa' Smith, previously Lord
Rothermere's chauffeur, had been given a car to set him up in business
and he was therefore taken on to ferry girls to and from the station. Tom
Busby, previously valet to Lord Goshen, became the school butler, whilst
Jack Purver, who had been in charge of grounds and gardens for the
previous owner, stayed on, remaining with the school for another forty
years. When I arrived at Benenden in the autumn of 1927, there were
already some 200 pupils after just four years and there was nothing
noticeably uncompleted about it. The first girls moved in to the new
house in January 1925. Initially there were just three houses Guildford,
Etchingham and Hemsted, and fees were £57 a term, which was quite a
lot for those days.

The three co-founders, all in their early thirties, were the first
Housemistresses. Miss Sheldon, who had the soundest academic back-
ground, was head mistress and head of Guildford; she also taught
English. Miss Hindle, the most practical of the three, was head of
Etchingham and taught mathematics; she also acted as school bursar
and took over as estate manager. Miss Bird, who at thirty-one was the
youngest of the three and had the least academic qualifications, was
Hemsted's Housemistress; she had however trained at Dartford College
of Physical Education and had taken a number of teaching courses in
Divinity. To start with, therefore, she took charge of games and gym.
Later, when a games mistress was appointed, she specialised in Current
Affairs and Public Speaking; she also took a special interest in the much-
loved weekly School Service. Miss Bird, or 'Birdie', as she became
universally known, had, before going to Wycombe Abbey, taught briefly

Another view of Benenden

at St. James' West Malvern where my older sister had been at school and had already met my mother; this no doubt was why the House chosen for me was Hemsted.

As the years rolled by the other two Founders became more and more involved in school duties and could no longer give undivided attention to those in their Houses. Birdie's particular interest, however, was people and until she retired in 1954 she continued to give special attention to girls in her House. Her philosophy was that everyone should succeed at something, and to this end she instigated the annual Hobbies Exhibition which became a very special feature of the school. Everyone in the school had to contribute something to the exhibition, my contribution invariably being even-weave linen embroidery and I still have a table cloth for which I was awarded a 'double-first.' One year I also accompanied on the piano an able violinist who had entered a solo piece as her contribution to the display. By the time, long after my day, that Birdie retired she had become a very special and well-loved Housemistress.

By the time I arrived at Benenden in 1927, two more Houses had been added, Medway headed by Miss Owen-Jones and Norris headed by Miss Summerhayes, the games mistress. Apart from the fact that my parents wanted the girls in the family to be educated so that they could earn their own livings, a strong reason for choosing Benenden had been that two of my mother's turn-of-the-century school friends lived nearby. One was Bessie Hall whose husband had been killed in World War One and who lived at Birchley, a comfortable house in nearby Biddenden where there was a tennis court, a live-in butler and housemaid, who I believe married when Bessie died, and a chauffeur. The other neighbour, who at the time lived in Rolvenden, was Daisy Morley, mother of Robert who at the time was just starting out on his career as an actor. During the five years I was at Benenden, half terms were invariably spent at Birchley, the chauffeur being sent to collect me and any friends I cared to bring from school. Some twenty-five years later when I came to live in Berkshire, the Morleys I found were my near neighbours and our contact was renewed.

As to school work I have surprisingly few memories, but from the start work was, as at schools now, allied to exams. The first exam I took shortly after I arrived was called 'Junior Oxford,' and after which one prepared for 'School Certificate'. Games were an important part of life at Benenden and were something I particularly enjoyed. In winter we played lacrosse and in summer tennis. Each House had under-fifteen teams as well as first and second teams. There were also School teams for matches against other schools. School matches were played on a Saturday, alternately at home and away. The names of those chosen for school teams were posted on a notice board on the Friday before the match. This was where, if you were hoping to be included, you learnt whether you had been selected for the team; or if you had played before, had been dropped, resulting in jubilation or mortification. Inter-house

Lacrosse matches were played during the week in normal games time and were taken very seriously, the whole house turning out to watch and cheer on their team, and to be the overall winner was a matter of considerable pride. By the spring of 1929 I had been made captain of the under-fifteen team and at one time or another played in all my house teams. I was even made House swimming captain, but being used in the holidays to swimming in the sea the fresh water pool did not appeal to me so I didn't do much swimming. By the time I left school I was playing in both the School and House lacrosse and tennis teams, ending up as what was called School Captain. In this position you were both head of the team and also in on team decision making, which I was happy to do.

Although I enjoyed playing almost any game, tennis was the one I particularly enjoyed. This had come about because my sister, five years older than me when she left school, lived at home and spent much of her time playing tennis – at which she was very good, one year being well placed at Wimbledon. During the summer holidays seaside towns from Paignton to Exmouth all hosted annual grass court tennis tournaments. My sister would play in these, usually winning a number of the events. She also played for Devon County which at that time, headed Group 1 in the Women's County ratings. In the winter she stayed with friends overseas in Athens, Singapore and India, played in their local tournaments, invariably coming home with cups or other prizes. But as prize money could not be given to amateurs, competitors had to bear all their own expenses, so the cost of her travels must have been heavily subsidised by our parents. At home my sister had her own car and in the summer holidays, I would go round the tournaments with her, playing in junior events, often having long waits for her before returning home. Devon at that time was very tennis-minded and had good men's and women's County teams. Devon was lucky in that Roberts, one of the best tennis coaches, taught from the Palace Hotel in Torquay and was always available to locals both for coaching and advice. Locally junior tournaments were laid on even for 'under twelves'. It was not surprising therefore that at Benenden, tennis was my favourite sport.

But to go back to work. I took my School Certificate exam in July 1931, passing with credits in English, French, Mathematics and Chemistry but failing to get a credit in History, a subject I disliked.

I remember my mother saying that she couldn't understand anyone not liking history as it was so interesting. Perhaps it was something to do with the way it was taught – or the fact that for the exam we seemed to keep going back over the history of the French Revolution! By then I was already being pressed into trying for a place at Oxford for which five credits were required. This also called for a credit in Latin, a subject I had for some reason been allowed to drop. If I was going to try for Oxford I would have to take up Latin again, so in July the following year I took Latin as a single subject and got my extra credit.

The next hurdle was the Oxford entrance exam. My best subject, and about the only one I enjoyed, was Maths which at that time was a subject few women took up. What I didn't know, and I am sure my teachers wouldn't have known either, was that at Oxford I could have taken engineering, something to which I would have been better suited as Meccano was my favourite toy. I left Benenden at the end of the autumn term in 1932, and was put on the waiting list for Lady Margaret Hall, but, when offered a place at St Hilda's, I accepted that. During the summer I stayed with my married sister in London and under tennis coach Vivien Glasspool, did the odd bit of tennis coaching in London. I went up to Oxford in the autumn of 1933.

So what had Benenden done for me? I had learnt about the importance of exams and passing them. It was thought that anyone who could make it should go on the University, but there the planning stopped. What you might do after you got your degree and the job it might lead to was never discussed. This was probably not the fault of the teachers, for the age of the 'professional' and especially of 'professional' women was still a long way off. You learnt to live with others, to conform and respect their views. Decisions made by one's elders were rarely questioned for the age of questioning everything had not yet arrived. If one's parents or school teachers said something was to be done this way or that, that was the way it went. Standards drilled in by a public school are for the most part still good ones; self discipline, respect for authority and for one's contemporaries and an ability to use one's free time usefully. Those you lived with were all of similar background and, as there was no mixing with those from other types of school, it did little to prepare you for the world to come – but the war would change all that. For me,

Benenden was to some extent a bitter-sweet experience as, until I became House and School Captain when I thoroughly enjoyed being a leader, I never completely fitted in.

In my last report my Housemistress wrote, "We shall miss Lettice very much in the House – she sets a very high standard for herself and others and has been a good and forceful House Captain". I was extremely competitive. To me second place at anything was a failure. This, psychologists might say, was something to do with being the middle child in a large family, plus the fact that my sister, five years older than me, used to bring back from her school lists of numerous positions she held from head of school downwards and I felt I had to live up to this. But Benenden was a glorious school and I am still very grateful to my parents for sending me there. If I had been sent to St. James' I would have been even more out of place. I was already longing for more professionalism. I wanted to be told the right way to do everything.

CHAPTER 4

OXFORD

When I got to Oxford I found that the situation as regards women and Maths was almost as bad there as it had been at Benenden. There was only one other person taking Maths and we did not have a tutor in College. Once a week I would bicycle up the Woodstock road to see a brilliant woman Maths tutor from LMH called Dr Winch, who would give me homework and direct me to the University lectures I should attend. Without anyone to discuss it with, the homework was often beyond me and on my next visit, her eleven-year-old daughter would be brought out to explain; this was not exactly a boost to my morale! I also remember sitting in the back row of a lecture room in University College listening to a lecturer called Hodgkinson on Calculus. Benenden may have taught me enough to get into college, but it certainly hadn't given me a grounding for what was to come next!

So as at Benenden it came back to games. As at Benenden one tended to stick with the minority of others who came from Public Schools. Apart from difference in interests, a reason for this was that those who came up on grants had to work harder in order to justify them, had less free time and probably less money – although my private allowance for the term was, unbelievably, only £15. There were no regular women's inter-college matches although there were three other women's colleges at the time, but my first summer I played in the Women's University tennis match against Cambridge and the following winter played for Oxford against Cambridge at Lacrosse. I had by this time made friends with a girl a year senior to me in the college who was captain of the university women's fencing team and I had decided that I too would like to take this up. This I did and in October 1935, when my friend went down, instructor Sammy Cromarty-Dickson wrote to me saying he hoped I was going to continue fencing and, if so, must be captain. He added, "… and we can arrange about a secretary and other officers . . ." So I took over as captain of the Oxford University Women's

Oxford and Cambridge University Women's Lacrosse Teams 1935, ELC back row 2nd from left. Betty Williams (Rendel), also from Benenden, back row 4th from left.

Fencing Club for the year 1935-6, winning the annual match against Cambridge. In the summer of 1936 I was also captain of the Oxford University Women's Lawn Tennis Team which that year beat Cambridge by sixteen matches to one.

Meanwhile, during the Hilary term of 1935, St Hilda's College Dramatic Society of which I was not a member, had enticed me to take part in their ambitious production of Clemence Dane's Wild Decembers. Staged in the Taylorian, my part was that of Emily Bronte, the eldest of the three sisters. In spite of the all-woman cast the local paper gave it a favourable report saying that of the three Bronte sisters Charlotte was perhaps the most outstanding though Emily, "played by Miss Lettice Curtis and Anne played by Miss Evelyn Job were hardly less commendable".

I sent a copy of this cutting to my father and received a reply which included, "What great pleasure it would have afforded your mother and I to have seen the production by the Saint Hilda's College Dramatic Society of Clemence Dane's Bronte play Wild Decembers.

It would indeed have entertained us greatly. Your success in getting into the Lacrosse team is very satisfactory. Lacrosse, fencing and tennis should suffice for recreation." The letter ended: "N.B. a Bank of England pound note enclosed."

This was my first and last appearance on any stage. In the May 20th 1935 edition of the university magazine Isis, my picture appeared with those of four men and one other woman under the heading "MEN AND WOMEN OF THE YEAR". This was followed in the edition of 10th June by an article nominating me as "ISIS IDOL." Even if I wasn't much good at Maths I had at least made some contribution to the University.

I discovered the other day some scraps of paper showing my expenses for October 1933, my first term at St. Hilda's; these included: JCR sub 17 shillings and 6 pence, library subscription 2s/6d, cap and gown 10s/6d, bicycle lamp, reflector and saddle cover 5s/3d, hair cut 1s/6d. Expenses for the week 6th to 12th November included: gramophone and needles at £3-16s-0d, records 5s/8d, a glass dish for 2d, a playhouse ticket for 3s/0d and a Flanders Poppy for 1s/0d.

I left Oxford at the end of the summer of 1936 and set off with Joan Lovegrove (Carter), a friend in the same year at St. Hilda's, to Vancouver where her father, Captain of a Canadian Pacific liner, was on the Vancouver to Japan route. Joan was joining her parents for the summer holidays and I had been invited to go with her as a travelling companion on the journey. We boarded the Canadian Pacific steamship *S.S. Empress of Britain* at Southampton on July 4th 1936. This took us to Quebec, from whence we took the train to Montreal; there we joined the now sadly defunct Trans-Canada railway for the journey to Vancouver.

The journey took five days and on the way across Canada we stopped off at Lake Louise in the Rockies. The descent from there to Vancouver presented us with memorable views. The Lovegroves lived in North Vancouver; the bridge connecting it with mainland Vancouver was not as yet built. Their house was at the foot of Grouse Mountain from which at night, large bears came down to raid the dustbins; Joan and I would go out at night hoping to see one – but we never did! During our stay we made a number of outings, the most memorable one to Vancouver Island. A ferry took us plus car to Victoria, from whence we hired a cabin on a beach. We slept in our sleeping bags on the beach and swam in the dark. We toured the Island and on the west coast watched logging and tree trunks rolling down the hillside into the water from whence ships loaded them.

Back on the mainland we visited Mount Baker and Bellingham, where from the Hotel Leopold I still have a menu which lists 'Leopold's extra cut N.Y. sirloin steak, fresh mushrooms, french fried potatoes, combination salad, coffee, rolls' all for the price of $1.25. Two T-Bone steaks cost $2.10 and wild blackberry pie 15c. We also visited Mount Ranier, a mountain of some 14,500 feet in the United States south of Seattle, staying at the Paradise Inn.

Whilst in Vancouver I was introduced to a Mrs Edgecombe and her son Stuart who was hoping to become a professional singer. To this end he had booked in for singing lessons with Allen Ray Carpenter, a well-known singing teacher in Pasadena. Amazingly, when he suggested that I join him there no objections were raised, so to Pasadena I went and, on the way down the coast, stopped off for a couple of nights in San Francisco with the parents of an old school friend. In Pasadena, Stuart and I made many expeditions, not the least memorable of which was one to the Mount Wilson observatory where we saw a man hand-grinding an enormous lens. We made use of the Pasadena Memorial Golf Course, visited the Forest Lawn Memorial Park in Glendale and the Coconut Grove in Los Angeles.

Soon it was time to consider how I was going to get home. The cheapest way, I eventually found, was to sail on a German cargo ship which carried a few passengers. There was one due to leave Los Angeles for Hamburg shortly before Christmas, which they said could drop me off at Rotterdam, from whence I could get a ferry to England. The ship was the *Norddeutscher Lloyd Elba* of just over 9,000 tons. I joined the ship with about a dozen other passengers in late December. We sailed down the coastlines of Mexico, Guatemala, Salvador, Nicaragua, Costa Rica and Panama until we reached Balboa at the entrance to the Panama Canal. We had stopped here and there en route to drop passengers, and by the time we left Balboa I was the only passenger. The crew consisted of the captain (who I rarely saw), the first officer, the engineer and a doctor who I saw the most of as he had little to occupy him. They all spoke, and wrote, excellent English and I very much enjoyed our passage through the locks of the canal which was in good weather.

But once in the Atlantic the weather became stormy. On the way over we celebrated both Christmas and the New Year and I still have a memento given me for Christmas by the crew. I disembarked at Rotterdam on the 5th of January 1937 and caught the ferry to England.

CHAPTER 5

LEARNING TO FLY

Back at home after this memorable holiday I immediately gave my mind to getting a job.

The appointments board at Oxford provided no help. All they suggested was spending another year at Oxford on a teachers' training course. This had no appeal for me and, anyway, I had no intention of putting my family to the expense of another year at university. The same applied to an idea I had to becoming a chartered accountant. This I seem to remember called for up to three years' training for which, in the early days, one was not paid at all. The rest of the jobs they had on offer were ones calling for a First Class degree. I remember going to Foyles, the premier bookshop of the time, asking about a job selling books, but had no luck. Even before I had left Oxford, I had become very conscious of the amount of money my parents had spent, and were still spending, on my education and was restless for the day when I would no longer be the burden I felt myself to be on their finances. We were a large family and there were three behind me all at public schools, including a brother at Eton. I was determined to stand on my own feet but for females, life was not that easy.

Then something happened which, in retrospect, altered the course of my life. I was driving back from Exeter in the baby Austin which we used to get us around, when on the Exeter-Newton Abbot road I passed Haldon airfield.

My only experience of aviation was spending 5/- on a joy-ride when Cobham's Air Circus came to Oxford, but this left no lasting impression on me. Aeroplanes had, however, already come into my life. In the mid-thirties, with the arrival of light aircraft and private flying, 'aviation for all' in this country was born. Major towns up and down the country were opening aerodromes and Torquay, not to be outdone, had decided it should have one too. Lying between Dartmoor and the sea there were few fields suitable for an airfield and so it was that the best Torquay council could find was a small and not too flat field between

Denbury and Ogwell, within a mile or two of our house. This was run by Provincial Airways and was opened, a local paper recorded, on Saturday April 10th 1935 by the Mayor of Torquay, Mr A d'Espiney. Amongst the celebrations was a parachutist, and a picture in a local paper showed him landing in a tree. The Aeroplane magazine recorded that getting to the new aerodrome meant driving through three miles of intricate Devonshire lanes. I was not at home for this event, but must have heard about it.

Thus when I drove past Haldon I would not have been entirely new to aeroplanes and diverted to a side road round the aerodrome, I stopped at a gate overlooking the field. Haldon was a basic landing ground for Teignmouth, with at the time, no clubhouse, hangar or other facilities. But whilst I was hanging over the gate an aeroplane appeared, circled and landed. The pilot taxied around looking for someone to advise and, with me the only person in sight, taxied over to where I was with his query. As a visitor myself I could not help him but during our conversation I asked him whether women could also be pilots and, getting a positive answer, left with much on my mind. This, I thought, seemed an active occupation infinitely preferable to sitting in an office – but how to set about it?

Arriving home, I made no mention of my thoughts to my parents but next time I was in town bought aviation magazines with advertisements from flying clubs giving the costs of learning. If I was to learn to fly I would have to earn a living at it, which would involve getting a commercial 'B' pilot's licence. We had each been left £100 in our grandmother's will and this was the way I decided that I would spend it. For learning to fly I selected the Yapton Flying Club at Ford, notably because it was the cheapest, the Wiltshire Flying Club at Thruxton coming second. It was now time to break it to my parents and I remember my father, who I expect knew more about aeroplanes than I did, saying, "I suppose you will come and knock the chimney-pots over," before retiring back behind his Times.

Before I started flying I took the precaution of taking the required 'B' licence medical. It would have been pointless for me to spend a lot of money learning to fly if I couldn't earn a living at it. For this I had to appear before the RAF's Central Medical Board. Some years later when renewing my licence I was given my file to take from one specialist to another and, returning to the waiting room with it, I couldn't resist taking a peep at it; the first entry was a summarised report of my first medical, which concluded that I was far too nervous ever to become a pilot! Having never had a medical before, it does not seem surprising that the august surroundings and strange procedures such as blowing up mercury and holding one's breath for 60 seconds had unsettled me! But they passed me and I continued with my plan.

So it was that in early June 1937 I found myself at Ford where I had been booked in at the Burndell Kennels, within walking distance of the airfield. Here Miss Ashdown, who bred Lakeland and Kerry Blue terriers, provided me with bed, breakfast and supper. My first 30 minute flight took place on 16th June 1937 in Cirrus Moth G-EBZC, instructor W.J. Alington.

Before applying to the Air Ministry for even a private pilots' licence you had first to get from the Royal Aero Club an Aviator's Certificate. This was a small navy-blue leather-bound document which stated that you had fulfilled all the conditions stipulated by the *Federation Aeronautique International* (FAI) who laid down the rules. For private pilots travelling abroad this was often treated as a passport as it included a photograph of the holder and, in six languages, this sentence: "The Civil, Naval and Military authorities, including the police, are respectfully requested to aid and assist the holder of this certificate". My Aviator's Certificate is No. 15099 dated 10th July 1937 and is signed by Lindsay Everard, Chairman of the Royal Aero Club and Harold Perrin, the Secretary. To obtain the certificate you had to pass an oral technical exam, in which you were asked some sixty questions, and carry out the following flying tests in the presence of a Royal Aero Club approved observer:

(1) A flight without landing during which the pilot shall attain a height of not less than 6,000 ft. The descent from this height shall finish with a glide, the engine being cut off at 4,500 ft above the landing ground, and the engine shall not be used again until the machine has come to a stop on the ground. The landing from this flight shall be made within 150 yards of a point fixed beforehand by the observer. The landing shall be made to the satisfaction of the observer who will indicate in his report in which way it was made.

(2) A flight without landing around two marks 500 yards apart making a series of five figure-of-eight turns, each reaching one of the marks. The turns shall be alternately to the right and the left. During this flight a height of not more than 600 ft shall be maintained. The landing shall be made by cutting off the engine not later than the moment when the machine touches the ground – it may be cut earlier – and by bringing the machine to rest without further use of the engine within 50 yards of a point fixed by the candidate before starting.

During these tests a barograph was carried and the observer had to sign the resulting trace thereon and submit it with his report. This done, the Royal Aero Club issued an Aviator's Certificate which one sent on to the Air Ministry enclosing five shillings, for which an 'A' Licence was issued. Mine, dated 16th July, allowed me to make cross-country flights and move on to 'B' Licence tests which called for a minimum of 100 hours solo flying.

There were, therefore, now 100 hours solo to be completed before I could apply to take the 'B' Licence tests. One of my early cross-countries was to Rochester to pick up Rupert Alington, brother of the chief instructor W.J. Alington – known as 'Marmie' – who was in the Navy. On arriving back at Ford I made a somewhat heavy landing; possibly I hadn't allowed for the extra weight. Next day I was back on dual again with his brother, the chief instructor! A junior instructor I now often flew with was 18-year-old Dennis Holland who died three years later in the Battle of Britain. A member of the RAFVR, when war came he was posted to No. 72 Squadron at Acklington. In September 1940, he was flying from Biggin Hill when he was forced to take to his parachute and on his way down was shot at by the German he had been chasing. He subsequently died in hospital.

During August and September I accumulated hours towards the 100 hours solo necessary for the 'B' licence. What I had not allowed for when I started flying in high summer was that I would be taking the tests which, when started, would have to be completed in three months, during the bad weather and short days of winter.

The Cirrus Moths I was flying at Yapton were very basic, they had the Cirrus II engine which was rated as 75 HP, and little instrumentation; only a compass, a vertical bubble for judging climb and descent,

A de Havilland Cirrus Moth.

and a horizontal bubble. These, therefore, were the instruments with which in October I started 'blind' flying dual at Yapton where a hood was put over the cockpit to prevent you from seeing out. After a couple of 'blind' dual trips with Dennis Holland, I continued flying with anyone I could persuade to come with me as safety pilot. This more often than not was Bill Mayo, a relatively experienced pilot who had left the Navy and was also working for a commercial licence at Yapton. I recall that as I got more confident I would sometimes climb through cloud on my own and fly above the clouds - though I doubt if I admitted as much to my instructors! There were also other things to practice such as cross-wind and 'rumble' landings, in which you had to keep the engine on until touchdown.

Three official cross-country flights had to be made, two by day and one by night. The only practice for the latter which I can find in my log book consisted of 30 minutes landing over car headlights at Yapton. All cross-countries had to be started at Croydon, where a barograph was fitted to show that no unscheduled landing had been made en route.

I took my first cross-country test on 26th November in radioless Cirrus Moth G-EBUS. The required route was Croydon-Hamble-

Cardiff and back to Croydon which, at some 80 mph or less on a late November day, was a good day's work. All went well until I approached Cardiff, where there were obvious signs of an approaching front. I managed to land and get my form signed before the airfield closed. When returning, on the other side of the Severn there was already cloud on the hills and I was forced to climb. I flew above cloud for over an hour, after which thankfully, the ground appeared below me. It was now rising three o'clock on a murky November afternoon but I pressed on, the main incentive being that if I failed to complete the test, I would have to pay for it all again. Eventually Worcester Park gasholder came into view – its name written on the top – followed by Croydon Airport with the large red letters QBI lit on the control tower. This meant that the visibility was less than 1,000 metres and the Control Zone was in force. This also meant that permission had to be obtained before landing, something only possible for radio equipped aircraft. But with fuel running short and in deteriorating visibility, I had no option but to land. I was told to report immediately to Jimmy Jeffs, the Chief Air Traffic Control Officer, in the control tower. In no uncertain terms I was told that I had entered the Control Zone without clearance, and had

Yapton Flying Club 1938/9

L-R; Bill Mayo, unknown, Dennis Holland (Shot down 1/9/40), Les Stonhill, Benge, ELC, 'Dutchy' Holland

made a Heracles 'go round' again. There was no possibility of getting back to Ford that night, or the next day either; but in spite of my entering the Control Zone they passed my test.

But there were other cross-countries which had to be completed. On January 6th I set off on a route Croydon-Lympne-Hamble, but on the return failed to find Croydon so turned south and force-landed in a field near Newhaven. A night flight was also called for which had to be undertaken on a moonless night, and as I should have been at Croydon, the flying club had arranged for me to do this the same night. So I was picked up by car from Newhaven and taken back to Croydon where Dennis Holland was waiting for me. It had been arranged for him to fly with me to Lympne demonstrating the route which I would take when flying solo back to Croydon. We left for Lympne at 8.30 pm with Dennis pointing out the odd beacon to guide me on my return. It was a reasonably clear night, but there was a strong wind. I set off from Lympne on the planned course to Croydon but the beacons I had been told to look out for did not appear; there was obviously more wind than we had allowed for. After about half an hour the Thames appeared beneath me. The only cockpit lighting in the Moth was from a hand-held torch so there was little chance of studying the map. Correcting course brought me over central London where there were lights everywhere similar to the Croydon beacon. I was just about to give up and turn south towards the coast when another possible beacon appeared which, happily, turned out to be Croydon. I landed at ten to midnight after a flight of one hour and thirty minutes; this was fifteen hours after leaving Ford in the morning and I had been in the air for over eight and a half hours. In the days before World War Two when a number were qualifying for their 'B' licences, I was by no means the only one to have problems with my winter cross-countries and night flights.

There was also practice to put in for the flying tests which had to be taken with No. 24 Communications Squadron at Hendon. The RAF Tiger Moths at Hendon were significantly different aircraft from the Cirrus Moths I was flying at Yapton. The Gipsy Major in the Tiger was rated at 130 HP, there was also a difference in instrumentation, for the Tiger Moths had a luxuries such as a turn and bank indicator which I had never used before. My first visit to Hendon for the General Flying Tests was on December 8th. Not surprisingly I failed the test.

Yapton Flying Club. ELC, Benge and Holland admire a new car!

Arrangements were therefore made for me to have a few hours with the London Aeroplane Club at Hatfield where the school had Tiger Moths and here I polished up both my general and blind flying. It was the end of January before I returned to Hendon to retake the General Flying Test which I now passed. Two days later I took the Hendon navigation test. This included a 'blind' flying test in which the pilot had to take off under the hood and remain under the hood for two legs of a previously prepared triangular course. For the last leg of the test the hood was lifted and with reference to the map, the pilot had to identify the position of the aircraft and set course back to Hendon. When landing back the Tiger blew over, for which examiner Pilot Officer McLeod was held responsible, as landing was not part of this test! This, then, completed my 'B' licence tests and my flying with the Yapton Flying Club at Ford came to an end.

CHAPTER 6

C.L. AIR SURVEYS

My 'B' licence is dated the 1st April 1938, but nobody thought for one moment that I would get a flying job. In May, however, I was offered one by Charles Lloyd who owned a company called C.L. Air Surveys.

Lloyd had served with the Army in WW1, and when seconded to the RAF had been involved in survey work in Egypt. On retiring from the Army he had been involved in surveys of India, Burma and Africa. Lloyd now had a contract with the Ordnance Survey to photograph specified areas of England for revision of Ordnance Survey 25 inch maps. As well as flying, C.L. Air Survey's work called for sorting and examining photographs before passing them on to the Ordnance Survey. As the photographs were to be used for stereoscopic analysis, flying involved holding very accurate courses so that points on the ground would appear on two adjacent strips. To help pilots fly these courses, Lloyd had fitted two Puss Moths with 20 inch wide-angle lens cameras, radio, and a basic auto-pilot There was also a certain amount of ground work to be carried out sorting and putting the photographs together. I was taken on both for flying, and helping out with the office work.

Charles Lloyd of C.L. Air Surveys

The team when I joined included Charles Lloyd himself, who flew a Bellanca which he was also planning to use for photography, and Bill Mayo, who I had known at Yapton. There was also Maclennan, who was responsible for the design of the tank wherein the 300 feet of film on each roll was developed, fixed and dried without being touched by hand. In charge of ground engineering and aircraft maintenance was Bishop, a very experienced ex-petty officer in the one-time Royal Naval Air Service. From Maclennan I learnt a great deal about photography and later, when stuck at Edinburgh on an Army co-operation job, I bought a second-hand Contax camera, one of the top cameras of the day, and a number of filters for £25, at the time an excellent buy.

Charles Lloyd with photographer Mac (left) and a Puss Moth.

When I joined the company in early May 1938 it was based at Southampton, Eastleigh, but by the end of the month it had moved to Doncaster in preparation for mapping photography in the region. My first flights were as navigator in Bellanca G-ABNW, a single-engined aircraft with a Whirlwind engine which was fitted with wireless and an autopilot which Lloyd was assessing for air survey photography. By mid June I was flying Puss Moth G-AAXO, fitted with wireless, autopilot and camera, carrying out tests of its photographic capability; test flying was also being carried out by Bill Mayo in the second Puss Moth. By the end of June survey photography had started in earnest in the Scunthorpe area. Strips of film were now being produced for analysis, but difficulty was being experienced in maintaining the very exact courses required to produce the necessary overlap. In the meantime, whilst I got more skilled at the job which called for a lot of practice, Mayo did most of the photography and I was more generally used for communication jobs. There was also the problem of weather; inevitably, there were more days when the weather was unsuitable for photography than those when photography could take place, thus when the weather was right it was of the greatest importance that good photographs were taken. It was whilst we were at Doncaster that the Bellanca undercarriage collapsed during taxying; this must have been a serious setback for Lloyd but we carried on, making the best of the two Puss Moths. From Doncaster we moved on to Nottingham where we remained for around a month, and from there we moved up to Newcastle in July for a contract covering Seaham Harbour. For the winter of 1938 we returned to Southampton, where we remained until the weather improved in May 1939. In the meantime there was plenty of work to keep us busy in sorting, examining and joining up the photographs which were needed for stereographic use into strips.

In May we moved to a new base at York of which I have partic- ular memories – and photographs. Here a busy flying club was run by ex-RN Commander Croxford. Instead of having to find a local bed I lived very comfortably in the club house. Amongst the club members at the time were well-off aircraft owners Morgan Barwick and Bill Humble, who during WW2 was a test pilot on Typhoons and Tempests with Hawkers at Langley. I enjoyed many a game of table tennis with Bill and my log book shows that I went up with him in his Gipsy Moth G-AAWR for practice aerobatics! Whilst based at York, we moved temporarily back to Newcastle in order to photograph Seaham Harbour and it was whilst we were here that Bill Mayo, working in the hangar with what turned out to be a wrongly wired-up electric drill, was electrocuted. As an engi- neer, as well as their best pilot, this was a serious loss to C.L. Air Surveys and from then on, for good or for bad, I had to take a greater part in the flying.

Bill Mayo had been a particular friend since we met at Yapton when we were both taking commercial flying licences. He had left first and had got the job with C.L. Air Surveys and I have always felt that it must have been his influence that helped me get a job with them. To me therefore, his death was also a personal loss. I recall that immediately after his death I was called down to Croydon, and I still remember the long non-stop drive down in my two-seater Wolsey Hornet for which, out of my salary of £5 a week, I had by now saved the necessary £25 that it cost to buy.

Whilst we were at York, Lloyd had taken on a sideline job of both photographing and producing the maps of a stretch of the River Trent to show

Bill Mayo who was killed in a tragic accident.

where dredging was needed. Normally, once photographs had been sorted and checked to make sure that the necessary overlap had been obtained, they went on to the Ordnance Survey who were responsible for the final mapping. For this job, however, we carried out the low-level photography and also made a pukka survey with theodolites so as to tie the photographs up with points on the ground in order to make the map.

By June, with preparations for war already going ahead, civil aircraft were being taken on for what was called Army Co-operation work. This somewhat boring work consisted of flying up and down the same specified course for up to two hours, for gunners to practise aiming their anti-aircraft guns. I have no idea what aircraft owners were paid for use of their aircraft, but out of this I was given £1 an hour flying pay. This was extremely profitable as, during July and August, I did over a hundred hours flying.

At the end of August we moved south to Croydon. From here I had an Army Co-op run over London and odd jobs which, with war in the offing, were for the most part photographs of camouflaged build-ings. The weather during this period, however, was unhelpful for photography. On 28th August I was hanging around the airfield when Sir Neville Henderson arrived back from Berlin in Junkers Ju52 D-AXOS bringing the news that, in spite of Britain's threat of war with Germany if Poland was invaded, Hitler intended to go ahead with the invasion. Before the aircraft taxied in, waiting press-men were cleared off the tarmac. I can only think that the reason I was not asked to move, although I was standing nearby with my camera, was that I was thought not worth bothering about! I therefore took shots of Henderson climbing out of the aircraft and about to get into the waiting car. Nowadays these would no doubt have been worth a princely sum, but they have appeared only in a book about the history of Croydon Airport.

On 1st September all civil aircraft were impressed by the Air Ministry and allotted to a department called National Air Communications, for carrying out communications work on a national basis. The Puss Moths, we were told, must be taken to Weston Super Mare from where I got a lift back to Croydon in a de Havilland DH.84 Dragon of Air Dispatch to collect my car. Back at Croydon I drove up to London to photograph famous landmarks which, we thought at the time, must almost certainly be destroyed in the bombing which was expected to follow immediately after declaration of war. This came two days later, on 3rd September leaving me wondering what to do next. Charles Lloyd was recalled to the Army but before leaving, he had persuaded the Director General of the Ordnance Survey at

ELC in a C.L. Air Survey Puss Moth.

Southampton, Major General
M.N McCleod, to give me an
unofficial job in their research
department. Ordnance
Survey employees were at
that time principally
Royal Engineers, many
of whom were now
being called up for
more important work. Amongst
the senior officers leaving was one Captain
E.H. Thompson, who had designed an automatic
plotting machine for the War Office. The post I was given was
with Othmar Wey, who had come over from Switzerland with a new Wild
Stereocomparitor which was being used on an experimental basis, for
measuring and drawing contours from aerial photographs. The new
machine, with others such as the Thompson automatic plotter, had
been collected together in Southampton's old library which was where
I worked. I had taken a room nearby in what was then the Royal
Hotel overlooking a park, a very pleasant situation. In the hotel were
a number of retired Army officers, mostly Majors, who had been
recalled for war service. As they did not qualify for active jobs they
would have been at least in their late thirties. They no doubt had
boring jobs and none of them had their wives with them. As a result
they were happy to indulge in a game of billiards, or other entertainment, with me of an evening. When I left Captain Ainsley gave be an
Army Brooch, which to this day I still have.

CHAPTER 7

AIR TRANSPORT AUXILIARY (ATA)
NO. 5 FERRY POOL, HATFIELD

In June 1940 a letter arrived from Pauline Gower, head of the Air Transport Auxiliary (ATA) Women's Ferry Pool at Hatfield, saying that an urgent need had arisen for more ATA pilots, both men and women. She was therefore looking for more pilots for her ferry pool at Hatfield. As one of the more experienced women pilots not yet called up, I now felt that it was my duty to go back to flying. I therefore gave notice as from the end of June to the Ordnance Survey, where I was in no way an essential employee. As it happened, shortly after I left the old library in Southampton where I had been working was bombed, so my job would have ended anyway!

I drove up to Hatfield from Southampton in my Lancia Augusta CUW66, which I had bought for £100 from a C.L. Air Surveys colleague who, on the outbreak of war, sold his small car and retained his much more powerful Bentley – something which he must surely have regretted when petrol rationing was introduced shortly afterwards.

:LC and
Pauline Gower
in the cockpit of
n Avro Anson.

There were now seventeen pilots in the womens ferry pool at Hatfield, where de Havillands had allotted the 'girls' a wooden building on the south side of the airfield. Here in January 1940 the first eight women pilots had started work delivering Tiger Moths. Pauline, although an experienced pilot herself, did not take part in the ferrying, but supervised the pilots' work, dealt with Ministry queries and with Gerard d'Erlanger, overall head of ATA at the headquarters at White Waltham.

Since then three more pilots had been taken on: Lois Butler, wife of the Chairman of de Havillands, Amy Johnson, who had been flying a blood delivery service to Europe, and Grace Brown who had flown pre-war for Mrs Victor Bruce's airline Air Dispatch. A fourth pilot, Joy (Muntz) Davidson, had also joined them, but was killed in May with her instructor whilst being checked out on a Master at Upavon – an accident eventually attributed to carbon monoxide poisoning. All of these four were experienced pilots and all were married.

Hatfield 1940
L-R;
M Fairweather
J Hughes
M Gore
P Gower
M Cunnison
D Farnell
G Patterson
Standing behind;
H Bretherton -
Stapleton
Adjutant

The first of the newcomers to arrive in June were Ursula Preston, Margot Gore and Ruth Lambton, the only one of our group who was married, whose RAF husband was killed shortly afterwards. Next came Philippa Bennett, Audrey MacMillan, Audrey Sale-Barker, whom we called 'the Audries', myself and Mabel Glass. I had never before met any of the other pilots. Somewhere for me to live had been found in a lodge of a large house at nearby Essendon, where I was far from happy. At Southampton I lived in a hotel where there was always company in the evening. Here, once I got home I was completely on my own. After a week or so I moved to the Stone House, a small hotel on the opposite side of the road from the de Havilland factory where there was always someone around to talk to or have a drink with in the evening.

The 'older' pilots – those who were married or in their thirties – had more money and were more used to social life. Winnie Crossley (Fair), who was parted from her husband, had rented a house called Abdale, where she lived and put up a selection of other pilots. Philippa, who had an open MG, was living in a pub at Tewin; Ruth Lambton and Ursula Preston shared a rented flat near the Stone House. Amy Johnson was allowed to live near White Waltham and bring the taxi Anson over daily, as did Margie Fairweather whose husband was a pilot in No. 1 Ferry Pool there.

Arriving at Hatfield we were first given a flying check, in my case with Margaret Cunnison, a pre-war instructor and one of the original eight. I was then sent off to put in some solo practice and next day took a Tiger to White Waltham to collect Margie Fairweather, with whom I flew back to Hatfield.

Instructions for flying in the summer of 1940 were laid down by the Air Ministry as follows:

    (a) avoid interference with or confusion amongst the active or passive defences of the country.

    (b) avoid the risk of false air raid alarms

    (c) avoid the risk of being shot down by our own defences.

This amounted to flying for recognition purposes within sight of the ground, keeping strictly to routes in areas defended by balloons and avoiding areas sensitive to the ground defence. Later in the war, when the danger from hostile aircraft waned, these rules were less strictly enforced but in the early days of the war they were taken very seriously.

We were even issued with Verey pistols and were supposed to get the 'colours of the day' before each flight, rules which for ATA flying were not practicable. As a result of these rules, however, we were instructed to fly in 'gaggles' which we were told would enable us to be more readily identified by the ground defence. Flying in 'gaggles' entailed following on one another in formation which made keeping a simultaneous check on one's position on the ground difficult, something which was essential lest for weather or any other reason one became separated from the leader or – as happened from time to time – the leader herself got lost! The taxi aircraft which dropped us off at a collection point and collected us on conclusion of a delivery, consisted at this time of an Anson loaned from White Waltham and a couple of Fox Moths, Margie Fairweather usually being the Anson pilot. By now, much of the Tiger production had been transferred from Hatfield to the Morris Motors factory at Cowley, Oxford, so it was from here that most of us started our first ferry trips. My first delivery came on July 11th, when I was dropped off by the Anson at Cowley to pick up a Tiger for Kemble; my next delivery trip was a Tiger from Cowley to Sywell. In accordance with the rules, even on these short trips, we followed each other in pairs.

Shortly afterwards I was one of a group bundled into the Anson bound for Perth to bring Tigers back down south. The flight up north, which involved intermediate landings at Burtonwood and Silloth, took nearly six hours and when we arrived, in somewhat doubtful weather, the airfield was in the course of being obstructed for the night. We spent the night in an hotel in Perth and the next morning, after being delayed by low cloud, we set off in the usual gaggle for Carlisle, our first refueling point, a flight that took 1 hour and 50 minutes. The Tigers were all for different destinations, so at Carlisle the gaggle broke up, some setting course down the east coast and some the west. My Tiger was for White Waltham and I chose the west route where Liverpool Speke was agreed as the next refuelling point. By the time I had been refuelled at Speke it was 7.30 pm, too late for me to make White Waltham. Not wishing to night-stop in Liverpool, I decided to start on my way and land for the night at Tern Hill, where an RAF friend from my time at Oxford was instructing on Masters.

Gabrielle Patterson, the first female flying club instructor, and Grace Brown, a pre-war commercial pilot walk away from a Tiger Moth at Hatfield, 1940.

As soon as my aircraft was ready, therefore, I started out unaccompanied; free for the first time since I joined ATA to choose my own route and where to land. I reached Tern Hill around eight o'clock. As I picked my way past what were then unfamiliar landmarks of the Shropshire countryside, a feeling of contentment and well-being lacking in my new job so far began to flood in. The cockpit of the Tiger was my world, control of it lay in my own hands; this was an entirely satisfactory state of affairs and on that summer's evening I was happy indeed that flying had once again become part of my life. Phil, who had landed at Burtonwood instead of Speke, had joined me at Tern Hill. After a night at a pub in Market Drayton we proceeded on our various ways; Phil's Tiger was for Desford. Marion Wilberforce, who had stayed the night at Liverpool and whose Moth was for Hatfield, called in at Desford to pick Phil up. Phil, arriving at Hatfield, got hold of a Fox Moth and came over to White Waltham to pick me up, so we were back in time for lunch. Thus ended a trip typical of our early days at Hatfield.

When there was nothing to ferry, I would offer to go with Margie in the Anson; this was not just a joyride as it would involve helping with the manual retraction of the Anson's undercarriage which called for some 150 turns of a handle, awkwardly placed on the right-hand side of and under the pilot's seat. Raising the undercarriage was really hard work, so much so that pilot and 'stooge' normally shared the task, each taking 20 to 30 turns at a time.

Because we were flying only trainer aircraft the fact that it was the Battle of Britain had little impact on us. The fact that bombs were often dropped in the vicinity of airfields we were visiting, or enemy aircraft were shot down, merely added to the day's interest. One day Ruth Lambton and I had just delivered Tigers to Kemble and, as we waited to be collected, we were watching a pale outline seemingly crawling across a blue sky.

Suddenly Ruth called out, "Look, there is something dropping out of it!"

We both watched with interest for some moments whilst the distance between the aircraft and some small items widened, then someone rushed out shouting at us to run to the air-raid shelter. It was then that we realised that the small objects were bombs and yet still we did nothing! On a summer's day, in the middle of an expanse of English countryside, the probability of a bomb hitting us seemed utterly remote. In fact the bombs landed harmlessly in a nearby field adjacent to the airfield that no doubt had been their target. After they had fallen we were hustled into a nearby ditch to shelter, much to our irritation as we wished to continue on our way to lunch.

In early October 1940, the de Havilland factory at Hatfield was bombed. As this was our base there was an organised air-raid drill and on an a 'red' warning we had to evacuate our office and make for the shelter. As so often happened, the air-raid siren and the bombs came at the same time and one bomb fell very close to those running from our office to the shelter. Luckily the bomb did not explode on impact, otherwise amongst those lost could well have been Pauline Gower, our commander, who was nearest to the bomb at the time. One of the bombs, however, landed on a factory workshop and twenty-one people were killed with some seventy injured. The bombs had been dropped from around 100 feet and the pilot had machine-gunned workers running to the shelters. The pilot of the Ju88 did not get home; caught by the airfield anti-aircraft guns he crashed nearby.

The Junkers 88 that bombed Hatfield before being shot down some minutes later.

Later that month I experienced one of my most unhappy trips of the war. I had been given what was described on my ferry chit as a Hart from Silloth to Sealand, and I was to go up to Silloth in the back seat of a Master from Woodley, flown by Amy Johnson. There was always an element of fuss when a passenger was carried on a ferry flight in this type of aircraft because ballast weights and aircraft covers stowed in the spare seat for transit had to be removed. We did not get away until around two o'clock on this September afternoon. We made Silloth in one hop despite a rather narrow petrol margin which, watching the gauges from the back cockpit, I was somewhat uneasy about. We arrived without incident and, clutching my collection chit, I climbed into a van to be driven to a far dispersal. It was here that I discovered that the so-called Hart was in fact a 'boosted' Hind. I had never before flown an aircraft with a boost gauge, I had seen them in the Anson but had not asked what they meant. These were the days before ATA Pilots' Notes had come along, so I asked the inspector to go over the cockpit with me, but his only response was to withdraw the form we signed to say that we were competent to fly the type of aircraft we were collecting. This was no boost to my already sagging morale; the aircraft seemed, and was, enormous compared to the Tigers I had been flying and I would have given anything for an excuse not to go. But there were still two hours of daylight left and the weather, although overcast, was reasonable.

Arriving at the aircraft in the absence of anyone else, I asked the fitter one or two points about the aircraft, including whether it was necessary to use the mixture lever; he assured me that it was. I settled myself into the cockpit; after Tigers it seemed an immense height off the ground. The engine was duly cranked by a man with a long handle and somehow I managed to taxi out and get airborne. I looked at the airspeed indicator, which was showing an incredible 150 mph. I pointed the nose towards the sea so that I could follow the coast whilst sorting myself out and in no time I was settling down to cruise at 1,500 feet. For this I selected, for no particular reason as I was unfamiliar with a boost gauge, zero boost which in fact was a somewhat high figure. I then started, in accordance with the advice I had been given, to inch open the mixture lever. The engine spluttered so I quickly pulled the lever back, but I had been told I must use it; I was desperate. I tried the lever again and once more the engine faltered, so again I pulled the lever back. After all these years I can still visualize the grey breakers and the angry rocks of the Cumberland coast between Maryport and Workington as I saw it that afternoon. I can remember looking down and wondering whether engine failure and a forced landing in the sea might not be the way out of this nightmare situation. But continuing south my mind was diverted by deteriorating weather, bringing fresh worries as to where, if I couldn't reach my destination, I could land. The high speed made navigation

Hawker Hind

somewhat easier as landmarks came up more quickly and eventually I arrived at the Mersey, crossed the Wirral peninsula and arrived at the Dee estuary and Sealand. Like so many airfields at that time runways were being built there and, to land, I had to choose a spot amongst patches of concrete and piles of earth. By now a steady drizzle was falling and I had never before landed an aircraft with a cockpit so far above the ground! Result, a big bounce, but luckily it came to rest in one piece. On reporting to Air Traffic Control I was told that the aircraft was not for them, but for the Maintenance Unit at the strip on the other side of the railway – or 'Little Sealand' as we later came to call it. This was a grass strip with very poor approaches, at the end of which was No. 30 MU, a packing station where aircraft were crated for sending overseas.

"Would you mind taking it over?" I was asked. Certainly I minded! It was now rising seven o'clock on a wet and thoroughly unpleasant evening, and nothing would have induced me to get back into the aircraft that night. The aircraft was duly delivered to Sealand by a test pilot, only to be lost at sea on its way to 16 Elementary Flying Training School in South Africa.

Philip Wills tells a very similar story about his first flight in a Hart with what information he could pick up from the civilian ground crew at Hawarden. At 2,000 feet over the Welsh hills the engine suddenly stopped and, putting his gliding experience to good advantage, he force-landed on a small uphill slope. Due to inadequate briefing he had taken off on the reserve tank and failed to switch over to the main. This took place on Christmas Eve and Philip spent an unhappy Christmas – as did those who had to guard the aircraft – standing by at Cosford. But that was the way things were in the first year of ATA, before there were pilot's notes and things became better organised.

CHAPTER 8

MASTERS AND OXFORDS

In June 1940 Nos. 1 and 4 RAF Ferry Pools were still employing significant numbers of RAF pilots who, with a shortage of fighter pilots, were urgently needed for operational duties. It was at this stage that all RAF ferry duties were passed over by the RAF to the ATA. This called for a large increase in the numbers of ATA ferry pilots and it was as part of this expansion that the decision was made that women pilots should take on the task of ferrying all types of training aircraft, starting with the delivery of Masters and twin-engined Oxfords. To clear them for flying the new types it was decided that, like ATA men, they should take a short course with the Refresher Flight at RAF's Central Flying School (CFS) at Upavon.

By the time I joined ATA fourteen women pilots had already been cleared for flying Masters and Oxfords. All had passed out successfully with the exception of Joy Davidson, better known as Joy Muntz who was killed, as has already been mentioned, with her instructor in a Master.

My turn to go to CFS came in October. There were three of us on this particular course; Audrey Sale-Barker, Connie Leathart and myself. The commanding officer at CFS at the time was Arthur Donaldson, and Connie Leathart had for her instructor her cousin John Armour. My instructor was Flying Officer Stratton.

Upavon was on a hill some 750 feet above sea level. Rooms had been found for us in a large house in Upavon village on the banks of the Avon, and each morning we walked up the hill to the airfield. We lunched in the WAAF Officers' Mess which was on the camp. I particularly remember an attractive WAAF Officer named Jo Pippon, daughter of an RN Captain, because shortly afterwards she was killed by an enemy bomb whilst on leave.

We all found the CFS course pretty harassing; we were so unbelievably ignorant. Constant speed propellers, retractable undercarriages, as well as most of the instruments in our aircraft were entirely

Miles Master

new to us. We were given no separate technical instruction or written notes, so it was simply a question of remembering what our instructors told us.

My first dual flight in a Master included – not very helpfully according to my logbook – some aerobatics, the idea no doubt being to give one confidence, but there was little hope of that! After two hours and forty minutes dual I made two solo flights and it was then on to the Oxford. After two hours dual in the Oxford, which included some single-engine flying, I did an hour's solo and after a further flight check was passed out. After ten days we returned to Hatfield cleared to ferry both Masters and Oxfords.

On 7th November, a few days after returning from CFS, I was given a Master to take from Reading to Hullavington. The following day I took an Oxford from Hatfield to Prestwick, where No.4 ATA Ferry Pool had recently been opened. The main work of this Pool was to take over aircraft arriving from the south and to deliver them to

Airspeed Oxford

their destinations further north. We would therefore hand over our aircraft there and return south. Our long trips to Lossiemouth and Kinloss were now at an end.

Some people when in an unfamiliar aircraft would worry about the take-off, others, about landing. I was one of the latter; I therefore worried the whole of the $2^{1/2}$ hours it took to get the Oxford to Prestwick as to whether I would land it in one piece! However, apart from the fact that the side window jammed open and I was extremely cold, all went well. Joan Hughes, who had also brought up an Oxford, and I were offered a trip back in a White Waltham Anson flown by Douglas Fairweather, Margie's husband. As the alternative was a night train from Kilmarnock on which we might or might not get sleepers, we accepted gratefully. The trip, however, turned out to be one which we both had reason to remember.

It was four o'clock when we left Prestwick, and we got as far as Carlisle for the night. The next day's weather was appalling, but Douglas hustled his passengers aboard the Anson and took off, saying that instead of following the coast, he would show us the lakes. We therefore followed roads and railways to Penrith and plunged into the narrow valley between the hills towards Ullswater. Over the lake all but the bottom few hundred feet of the surrounding hills were in cloud. In those days I had implicit faith in any pilot who had more experience than myself but even so, I was far from happy with the look of things. Eventually even Douglas had to give up and, after a very low turn over the water, managed to extricate himself and return along the route by which we had come. Even when we returned to the coast there was only just enough room to scrape along under the clouds. Anyone else, if they had taken off at all, would have turned back, but Douglas, renowned for his bad-weather flying, got through to Hawarden and then eventually to White Waltham, where we spent a further night. We would in fact have been better off catching the night train!

Most of the Oxfords went north for storage at that time and so it was that after one night at home, I set off again in another one for Prestwick, this time with Philippa. But not far north we flew into a deep depression so we decided to land at Tern Hill where we spent the night. On arrival at Prestwick next day we were given for the return journey

Philippa Bennett and Winnie Fair.

two dilapidated Gipsy Moths, one for St. Athan and the other for Llandow, a matter of some five hours' flying. On our third day out, the two-hour flight got us as far as Blackpool from where, after some lunch, we again set off for our destinations. We did not follow each other on these trips, and so it was at about four o'clock on this November evening that I arrived over Staverton, doing a mental calculation as to whether I had enough fuel to make Llandow. Suddenly over the sound of the engine I heard a dull 'whoomp' and then another. Puzzled, I then saw puffs of smoke above me and realised that the airfield anti-aircraft guns were firing. Deciding to get out of the way as soon as possible I throttled back and landed. Once on the ground I was told that a German had been spotted flying across the airfield a few thousand feet above me – the reason for the anti-aircraft fire. Phil had pressed on and was already at St. Athan, somewhat scornful that I hadn't made Llandow. The next day, after delivering my Moth, I joined her at St. Athan, where in those early days there were no taxi aircraft to collect us. We therefore hitched a ride in an RAF Whitley which was going to Kemble, from whence we persuaded a visiting White Waltham taxi Anson to drop us at Hatfield. In the past seven days I had slept in places as far apart as Market Drayton in Shropshire, Prestwick, Carlisle and Cheltenham, after which one's digs felt like home indeed, and a clean set of clothes the ultimate luxury.

Phil and I went around quite a bit together at this time. With wartime petrol rationing, alternatives to work were strictly limited. Even when there were no aeroplanes to fly we had to remain at the airfield until at least midday in case some urgent movements came up. Both Phil and I found hanging around pretty irksome and we were always volunteering for jobs – sometimes when others were reluctant to fly. We would sometimes get similar ferry chits for up north out of reach of the taxi service, taking blank chits which we would fill in ourselves if there was another aircraft that required moving at a Maintenance Unit to which we had delivered our first aircraft. It was not unusual for us to be away for three or four days, the only requirement being that we phoned Hatfield every night, letting them know what aircraft we had moved. Typical of our outings was one in which we took Masters from Reading to Prestwick, and then got a lift to Dumfries where we collected a pair of Queen Bees for delivery to St. Athan. The all-male Pool at Prestwick must have been delighted to let us take these slow and cold aircraft off their hands.

The main areas between London and Prestwick which, because of balloons, had to be given a wide berth were Birmingham and Coventry; the narrow corridor through the Liverpool, Widnes, Warrington and Manchester balloon complex; and Crewe - which prevented us following the main north-south railway line. Further north there were balloons around Barrow-in-Furness which, in bad visibility, made crossing Morecambe Bay more difficult. On the east side of Birmingham there were balloons at Rugby, Nottingham and the Humber which had to be avoided. We usually chose the west-of-Birmingham route as this avoided the necessity to cross the Pennines. In those early days we were not allowed to mark either balloons or newly-built airfields on our maps, and wartime airfields showed no identity codes. Our maps were marked with our personal codes so that if we lost them –a breach of security – and they were handed in, the owner could be traced.

CHAPTER 9

WINTER 1940 TO SEPTEMBER 1941

The winter of 1940-41 was an appalling and comfortless one for flying. This was the period when the Germans, having failed to gain mastery of the air during the Battle of Britain, attempted to knock out Britain by massed night bombing after a brief respite during January and February when even the enemy had to bow to the weather. By January snow had set in, continuing on and off until early March.

On New Year's Day, a group of us were given Tigers and Queen Bees to take from Hatfield to St. Athan. Mine was a Queen Bee (T4746). The weather forecast was bad; Ann Douglas and Diane Farnell gave up and landed at Kemble. Connie Leathart and I managed to get there and were collected in the taxi Rapide by Philippa Bennett. After dropping off Connie at her pre-ATA stamping ground at Whitchurch, we landed at White Waltham short of petrol before returning to Hatfield. Next morning Winnie Crossley, Joan Hughes and I were flown in the Rapide to Reading to collect Masters for Ternhill. When we got there the aircraft

The Queen Bee, a Tiger Moth converted to be flown remotely as a target aircraft.

were not ready. This and local snowstorms delayed our departure until 14.30 when, in a break in the weather, we took off and went our separate ways. I followed the usual valley through the Cotswolds from Oxford to Morton-in-the-Marsh, and then turned left towards Worcester to avoid the Birmingham balloons. At Kidderminster, however, sky and earth merged into an amorphous greyness and, whilst I was still wondering what that greyness held, quite suddenly it was snowing. When you are committed to contract flying snow can be very frightening. Unlike rain, which you can normally see approaching, snow will appear quite suddenly and close both the route in front and behind at the same time. After a brief interval during which I watched the snowflakes approach the windscreen with apparent slowness, only to speed up at the last moment and follow the contour of the aircraft, I turned back to land at Little Rissington. At 750 feet on the Cotswolds it was already covered with snow. Joan and Winnie also turned back, but landed at Upper Heyford.

On arrival at Little Rissington I reported to the 8MU hut and then walked to the Officers' Mess to enquire about a bed. Sometimes when 'stuck out' we would get transport to a nearby town and end up at a local hotel, but I had not chosen well: at 'Little Riss' there was neither a convenient nearby hotel or any transport to get me there, so I had to settle for the WAAF Officers' Mess which, as ever, was some way from the main Mess. This, however, was already full up and all they could offer was the bed of one 'Ruth' who was on night duty. This at least meant that the bed was well aired! The heating in the house had broken down so it was incredibly cold. By the morning the water was frozen in the washbasins and my face flannel was stiff as a board.

The following day it snowed on and off all day. In spite of the hopeless forecast I went out to the Master which, not surprisingly as it had stood out all night, refused to start. At around 3.15 pm we eventually got it going but, at this hour on a winter afternoon with snowstorms still around, I decided it was too late to start out. There was no alternative but to return to the still frozen-up WAAF Officers' house where, this time, I was allotted the bed of a Mrs Davies. After yesterday's protracted efforts at starting, room had been found for the Master in a hangar. Just as well, if the jottings in my notebook can be believed, for there was 18 degrees of frost!

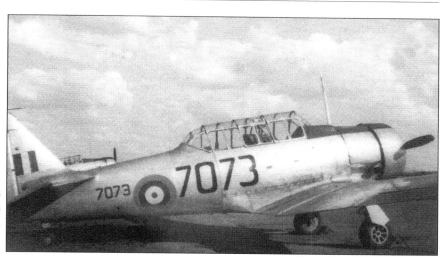

A North American Harvard in South Africa.

The next morning the snow had let up a little so I was able to make Ternhill at last, where I met up with Joan and Winnie. There were five other pilots there who had been flown up from Hatfield to collect a batch of Harvards, which the RAF school was replacing with Masters. Our job was to join them in taking the Harvards to Odiham, where they were to be crated for sending overseas to an Empire Training school in South Africa. This was only the second Harvard I had flown and I still wasn't that happy about it. The first one had come in December when some Harvards suddenly appeared on our books and a group of us had been sent to Little Rissington to collect them. At the time American aircraft had many features that we were not familiar with. In Spitfires and Hurricanes, for instance, there was a stop on the throttle which prevented over-boosting on take-off. In the Harvard there was no such stop, so on take-off the boost gauge had to be watched to prevent over-boosting. Another feature with which we were completely unfamiliar was the steerable tailwheel. In Hurricanes and Spits on take-off – or more particularly on landing – one could use full rudder, switching from one foot to the other to keep the aircraft straight. Full rudder now turned the Harvard tailwheel, so much more care was called for in its use – something that became even more evident when the Tomahawk came along. At Hatfield, cut off from more experienced male ferry pilots, we had no one from whom to seek advice about new types. As most of us had never before even seen a Harvard, a helpful test pilot at 8MU offered to give us circuits before leaving. A couple of our party sensibly accepted the offer, but one voice from our midst piped up saying: "No thank you, I'm quite confident." Although by the grace of God we all delivered our planes safely, it is perhaps of some interest to recall that this particular individual left ATA in early 1944 after a number of subsequent incidents! Although I felt far from confident, I was one of those who went off without the proffered circuit. My friend Philippa, whose Harvard was unserviceable, bravely came with me as a passenger. But to go back to Ternhill. My logbook shows that on my aircraft the connection between rudder bar and tailwheel was broken, not perhaps a disadvantage as on the ground one could use the rudder without danger of oversteering on landing. To add to my worries, once in the air I found that the ASI didn't work, but once again all six of us managed to deliver our Harvards safely.

The next day, Sunday, the weather reverted to its usual state of low temperature, snow showers and low cloud. Only Philippa and Marion Wilberforce took to the air that day, in Tiger Moths for Scotland; Phil, however, soon returned. With no flying possible I went to my garage, intending to give my Lancia Augusta an engine run. I had drained the radiator as anti-freeze was not generally available at that time, but the water I poured in simply disappeared then suddenly spouted out of the oil breather. On Monday January 6th, when we reported for work, we found that there was a 'flap' on with much

Amy Johnson who was posted missing on January 5th.

telephoning going on. Amy Johnson, it seemed, had been missing since the previous afternoon. She had been on her way south from what was, at the time, an unknown point of departure. I remember my disappointment when the party which had been laid on for that evening to celebrate the anniversary of the opening of the women's Ferry Pool at Hatfield had to be cancelled. The weather was still unflyable and there was nothing to be done by hanging around so I went back to my car. Pauline kindly lent our driver Pat Beverly her car to tow mine to the Lancia works at Wembley, where they found that freezing up had cracked the cylinder block. In the icy weather we had been experiencing I should, it seemed, have drained the cylinder block as well as the radiator.

On Tuesday there was still no flying. After reporting to the airfield I spent the rest of the day with Phil, lunching with her at the Rose and Crown at Tewin where she had digs, and afterwards walking to the Moat House for tea followed by a visit to the flicks.

Wednesday was yet another day of 'no flying.' A Canadian Army friend from my days at Southampton rang and as I was free, drove up and we had lunch in The Comet. Afterwards we went to the local cinema to see The Dictator and rounded the evening off at a dance that was taking place at the Stone House, the pub where I lived opposite the airfield. On Thursday, with the weather fit only for short trips, I took an Oxford from Hatfield to Cranfield. This time a group of us went to Abdale, the house rented by Winnie Crossley one of our senior pilots. After the inevitable walk we had tea and afterwards adjourned to The Comet where for some reason Winnie, who must have been celebrating something, regaled us with champagne. Wartime petrol rationing prevented us driving far afield for our entertainment!

On Friday morning I tried to get Wendy to Cambridge in the Puss Moth to collect her aircraft, but was prevented by cloud on the ground, so it was yet another day of no ferrying.

With the arrival at White Waltham the previous December of the BOAC Flying School, courses were started to teach pilots something about the technical aspects of the types of aircraft they were now being required to fly. In March, Phil and I were sent to White Waltham for what must have been one of the first of these courses. The instructor was BOAC engineer Bill Gribble; a who spared no effort in his attempt to get technical know-how into the heads of, what must have seemed to him, exceedingly dim, reluctant and ungrateful pupils. Reluctant because, instead of flying, we had to spend two weeks in a classroom.

"In two weeks," Gribble told us, "we can only hope to give you an appreciation of the principles involved, and not a complete understanding." This was the understatement of the year as we knew nothing about injection carburettors, hydromatic propellers or a mysterious instrument called an Exhaust Gas Analyser which was appearing in American aircraft. Lessons about airflow, reasons for slots, flaps and standard atmosphere went mostly over our heads but carburettor icing, grades of fuel and damage that could be done by mishandling engines was of more interest. For the course we had to put on skirts and black stockings instead of our more usual slacks, and had to carry gas masks. My main memory of the course is of arriving late one morning and missing the peg on which I was trying to hang my gas mask, with the result that the bag fell on the knob of a fire extinguisher, setting it off. Gribble, with characteristic presence of mind, rushed out of the classroom and pointed the extinguisher out of the window.

Back at Hatfield in the spring of 1941 there was still a government ruling that women must not fly operational types, but we were now told that we could fly 'obsolete' types. Thus in April I was given a

Westland Lysander

Lysander to deliver from Watford to Cosford. Shortly afterwards I had another one to take from Wroughton to Prestwick – a two-and-a-half-hour flight. Ones going to Prestwick at the time were en route to Aldergrove and later I took one the whole way. Unfortunately, my map blew out of the window as I was leaving the coast at Stranraer, but I managed to find Aldergrove without it.

The Lysander was an unusual aircraft, built to an Army Cooperation specification which called for exceptionally short take-off and landing qualities. Its high wing had full-span wing leading edge slots which clattered open automatically at 80 mph. The slots operated the flaps, which brought about a considerable change of trim. The result was that, when trimmed for landing, if the throttle was opened too rapidly on an overshoot the aircraft reared up, calling for urgent re-trimming. This was a most unusual aircraft, but one which I really enjoyed flying, sitting some seven feet up in a virtual greenhouse.

CHAPTER 10

HURRICANES AND SPITFIRES

For the women pilots at Hatfield, everything changed in the autumn of 1941. Up to this time there had been a government ruling that women should not fly operational types of aircraft, but in the summer of 1941 the war situation was as serious as it had been in 1940. With improved weather the blitz had started up again, and many thousands of people had been killed. The number of German U-Boats was increasing and shipping losses rising. In July there was a serious invasion scare and we were all given instructions as to what we should do in if the German's came; I received a note saying that I was to go to White Waltham to work as a taxi pilot.

The government-level decision must have come about from the necessity to make maximum use of every available pilot. At that time aircraft production was increasing and they had to be cleared from the factories where they were at risk of being bombed. BOAC pilots were about to be recalled to work for the Corporation and ATA were about to add to their commitments the bulk of the ferrying from Air Storage Units to Squadrons – a task still undertaken mainly by the RAF. We first heard of the changes on 19th July when Captain Henderson, the test pilot to the Technical Department at White Waltham, was tasked with bringing a Hurricane over to Hatfield for a few of us to do a practice landing. Here, four of the original eight girls did one practice circuit. Having by now flown Masters, Harvards and Battles they had no problems, but the rest of us had simply to get in ferry aircraft and fly them.

My turn came in less happy circumstances. Returning by night train from Kilmarnock after delivering an Albacore to Prestwick, my next task was to take a Dominie to Dumfries. I was told to ring the Ferry Pool at Prestwick when I had delivered the Dominie, and ask them whether they had anything for me to take south. When I rang I was told that there was a Hurricane at Dumfries that was required at Prestwick. I told the operations officer that I had not been cleared to fly

Hurricanes, to which he replied that women were now cleared to fly them – a notice to this effect must have been generally circulated! I felt that I had no option therefore but to accept the task.

Hurricane L1927 turned out to be an elderly Mark I, with a Merlin II engine and a power lever which had to be used as well as the normal selector to move undercarriage and flaps. With a host of butterflies in my stomach I climbed in, turned for the first time to the page labelled 'Hurricane' in my new Pilots' Notes and looked around the cockpit for the relevant levers and knobs. In due course I started up, taxied out and, to my utmost relief, got myself into the air without incident. The most disconcerting thing I found about it was that, being used to Masters, the forward view when taking off or landing was poor, but I was glad to find that in the air one had a better view. The trip up the Nith valley to Prestwick took only fifteen minutes. I managed to land in one piece at Prestwick, which was still a not particularly flat grass field, but I was not happy with my landing. I would have liked to have done a couple more landings, but there was far too much news value at the time in women flying Hurricanes, to risk any non-essential take-off or landing with a ferry aircraft. I got a lift with a pilot in a Hudson going to Ringway where I spent the night. Next morning I was offered a Fulmar from the Fairey factory, much to the surprise of the Fairey test pilots, which was for the packing station at Stapleford Tawney. Although in many ways similar to the Hurricane, it had better forward visibility and I found it pleasanter to fly and easier to land. At Stapleford a Magister had been left for me in which I flew back to Hatfield.

A week later I was given another Mk. I Hurricane from Hawarden to the General Aircraft factory at Hanworth, where it was to be converted into a Sea Hurricane by – amongst other things – fitting it with catapult gear and changing the airspeed indicator to read in knots instead of miles per hour. I had ferried eight Hurricanes and was just beginning to feel at home with them when I was given my first Spitfire. The aircraft, R5720, collected from the Morris Motors works at Cowley, was one of the few remaining Mk. Is in which the undercarriage was retracted by use of a hand-pump. This was something obvious to an

The classic lines of the Supermarine Spitfire.

No.5 Ferry Pool, Hatfield, May 41. L-R; Miss Connie Leathart, Mrs Lois Butler (in hat), Miss Margaret Cunnison, Miss Pauline Gower, Miss Jackie Sorour, Mrs Honour Salmon, Mrs Ann Douglas, Miss Anna Leska (Poland), Miss Barbara Wotulanis (Poland), Mrs Winifred Crossley (with gloves), Miss Lettice Curtis, Mrs Patricia Beverley (Driver - later pilot), Miss Audrey Sale-Barker, Miss Audrey MacMillan, Miss Rosemary Rees, The Hon Mrs K. Farrer (Adjutant).

onlooker as when the pilot pumped, the pilot's hand on the stick would move fore and aft in sympathy thus raising and lowering the nose.

In those early days, females landing in either a Hurricane or a Spitfire at an RAF or even an ATA airfield was inevitably a matter for some comment. We felt, therefore, that the less attention we drew to ourselves the better. This, however, was not always possible, as the following shows:

On the 21st August 1941, two weeks after my first Hurricane, Joan Hughes and I were sent off to Prestwick with two Magisters from Cowley. After refuelling stops at both Ringway and Kirkbride, we duly arrived there and spent the night in Ayr. Next morning, as was usual in those days, we asked the Ferry Pool if there was anything to take back south, and were given a couple of Canadian-built Hurricanes from Silloth. To get to Silloth we hitched a lift in a Hudson to Kirkbride and from there were taken in a Rapide to Silloth, where we arrived at about one o'clock only to find that the ground crew had gone to lunch; it was therefore after two o'clock before we could get away.

The Hurricane carried fuel for just over two hours' flying; just about enough to get us to Hatfield, but in those early days we were ultra-cautious and in any case the weather was not too good. There was low cloud and rain down the west coast, our usual route, so instead we decided to cross the Pennines and fly down east of the hills, refuelling on the way at Finningley, a large grass airfield near Doncaster. I took off first and went on my way via Penrith, Appleby and Barnard's Castle.

Joan took off almost immediately afterwards but when she tried to raise the undercarriage she was unable to move the selector lever. We were very conscious at the time that anything we did tended to be built up into a 'good story,' and Joan, afraid that if she returned to complain, they might attribute it to her small stature and lack of strength, put her foot on the lever and gave it a shove. It moved and the undercarriage retracted, but now she was unable to return the lever to neutral. Still struggling, she flew on to Finningley where I had already landed. From the ground I watched her approach the field and continue to circle, undercarriage retracted, her foot unable to help her move the lever from the 'up' position. The lever, working in an H-slot, was used to select flaps as well as the undercarriage, so these too could not be used. After circling for some time Joan had no option but to come in for a flapless belly landing in which the aircraft slid smoothly over the grass, with the propeller blades bent, but with virtually no other damage.

Confronted with the situation, Joan's main worry was what the Accidents Committee would have to say about it! Would she be blamed? Perhaps it was a little unwise to use her foot, and what would be the effect on women pilots flying Hurricanes as a whole? Would the incident be seized on by those always standing on the side-lines ready to say: "I told you so"?

But at Finningley the RAF, recovering from the surprise of two females arriving in Hurricanes, were all helpfulness. They refuelled my aircraft, took charge of Joan's, and even flew her back to Hatfield in a Hampden. Luckily all ended happily; Joan was exonerated by the Accident Committee and we continued to fly Hurricanes, progressing to Spitfires shortly afterwards.

A month later I was given an Oxford to take from White Waltham to Abbotsinch, returning to Prestwick where I once more spent the night. this time at the Orangefields Hotel on the airfield where the trans-Atlantic pilots congregated. The next day I was given a Mk. V Spitfire to take south: I had flown my first one only two days before. The weather, however, was unpromising. I hung around all morning, alternatively visiting the Met office and drinking cups of coffee, but there was little promise the Met could give. They said that the whole country was covered with an autumn haze and that down the west coast there was

Spitfire V approaching bad weather.

low cloud as well, so that route was definitely out. After lunch I decided that I could get as far as Kirkbride and after that, the 'actuals' from airfields the other side of the hills showed that there was at least a chance of getting down east of the Pennines, so I decided to have a go. I eventually got away at about three o'clock. From Prestwick I flew as usual down the Nith Valley to Dumfries, across the Solway Firth to Carlisle, and down the railway to Penrith and Appleby. Following the lower ground through the hills to Barnard's Castle I then picked up the main railway south between Darlington and Northallerton. It was hazy, but as long as I could make out the railway below me I could keep a check on my position and would be able to find a diversion airfield without too much difficulty if visibility worsened or the haze turned into low cloud.

Conditions remained much the same and, as one landmark after another turned up on schedule, I pressed on south, one eye on the petrol gauge, postponing as long as possible the decision whether to go on or land to refuel. By the time I crossed the A5 at Stoney Stratford I realised that I could make White Waltham and, being once more in familiar territory, set course direct.

It was around five o'clock when I came into the circuit. The flight from Prestwick had taken around two hours and my fuel was all but exhausted. The weather was still not particularly pleasant, but there was enough daylight to complete the delivery to the squadron on the south coast. After landing I took my ferry chit into the No. 1 Pool operations room and, because I thought it was expected of me, offered to take the aircraft on although starting out again was the last thing I felt like doing. Doc Whitehurst, deputy CO of No. 1 Ferry Pool, was in the Operations Room; he made no comment except to say that this would not be necessary, and returned to his office next door. With a surge of relief I handed over my ferry chit for signing and turned my thoughts to getting home for the night.

It was only some time afterwards that I learned that No. 1 pool had that day been 'washed out' after pilots who had taken off for the north had returned reporting that the weather was unsuitable. The arrival of a female pilot in a Spit from Prestwick had, I was now told, caused considerable consternation, especially amongst some of the American pilots who had turned back. But the incentive to get home was always stronger than the urge to set out with the likelihood of getting 'stuck out' and in any case, the normal west coast route had been impassable. Women pilots had only very recently started flying Spitfires and this was only the second I had flown. Quite possibly, therefore, this may have been the first Spitfire to be landed at White Waltham by a female which one imagines, would in any case have made it quite a talking point.

This was September 22nd 1941 and I arrived back at Hatfield next day to find that I, with some dozen others, was to move to Hamble at the end of the week. This was why we were being required to fly Spitfires.

CHAPTER 11

NO. 15 FERRY POOL, HAMBLE

In 1939, when the terms under which female pilots were to be employed was being discussed, the Treasury had ruled that women pilots could not as a matter of policy be paid at a rate equal to that of men doing the same job; this was contrary to civil service practice. Now in 1941, when more ferry pilots were desperately needed, salaries of women pilots were to remain unchanged although they must, in addition to the Spitfires, take on a greater range of aircraft. This would involve them joining and sharing the work of Ferry Pools that, to date, had employed only male pilots.

ATA was now training men and women pilots from scratch on an equal basis and was about to take on some women pilots from the United States. There were also other reasons for closing the Ferry Pool at Hatfield. The Mosquito, which had first flown in November 1940, was coming into production in ever-increasing numbers and de Havillands were anxious to get rid of their ever-expanding lodger unit. It was

Margot Gore

decided therefore that the more senior pilots from Hatfield would move to Luton, where a new *ab initio* training school was being set up and where they could advise and encourage the new pilots. A further group of eleven of us was to go to Hamble, where the major work at the all-male Ferry Pool consisted of moving Spitfires. Supporting tasks consisted of clearing Oxfords from Airspeed's at Christchurch and Portsmouth Aviation. Now that women pilots were cleared to fly both these types they could, it was decided, be capable of taking over the work of this Ferry Pool and turning it into a second all-woman Ferry Pool. The move came into effect on 29th of September 1941 when eleven of us from Hatfield moved down to Hamble, where Margot Gore had been chosen to be the new head of Pool, and Rosemary Rees her deputy.

In wartime, almost any house with spare rooms made them available as 'war work'. When we arrived, Phil and I had been booked rooms in Mere House, a comfortable home overlooking the Hamble. Phil eventually moved into a house in Sidney Cottages which she shared with Rosemary Rees, whilst I and two others moved to Southampton, booking in at the hotel I had lived in at the start of the war. Here there were 'red' air raid warnings, meaning aircraft overhead, for five nights following our arrival. Sometimes, strictly against the rules, I would go up on the roof in the evening to watch searchlights sweeping across the sky as they sought to pick up enemy aircraft, and the tracer bullets crawling up towards them. On a clear night it was an impressive sight. Occasionally there would be a 'crump' and a flash as enemy bombs descended, for the most part on the other side of Southampton Water, away from the balloons. Three male members of the original Ferry Pool remained to ferry types that we were not yet qualified to fly and to generally help us settle in; they couldn't have been more helpful. They cheerfully accepted Margot as their new Commanding Officer; they flew us around in the taxi Anson introducing us to their factories and Maintenance Units and, as well as being efficient, were really good fun. This was the first time any of us had worked alongside more experienced male pilots and, after the somewhat boarding school atmosphere at Hatfield where a limited amount of work had to be shared out, at Hamble there was plenty of work for all. We might get two or three short jobs a day; personally I found the change from life at Hatfield entirely stimulating.

The work at Hamble consisted for the most part of short ferry trips, many of not more than twenty minutes, from factory to Maintenance Unit. There were no more long flights up to Prestwick as aircraft for the north were now left at White Waltham for on-ferrying by pilots of No. 1 Ferry Pool. For the return journey, because of the proximity of Hamble to the Royal Naval stations at Worthy Down, Lee-on-Solent and Gosport, we were often given naval aircraft to collect from White Waltham, where they had been dropped en route. These aircraft included Gladiators to Gosport, Chesapeakes and Swordfish to Lee and Albacores to Worthy Down. On my fourth day at Hamble I flew my first Walrus, an amphibious aircraft that could be landed on land or water,

Supermarine Sea Otter, a later development of the Walrus

but not on the latter by ATA. Its appearance, like much else about it, was unique. It was a large, single engined biplane with a Pegasus engine mounted on struts between the wings and a pusher propeller that rotated aft of them. To some extent it was more like a ship than an aircraft. The crew sat in a roomy hull forward of the wings, entry being through the flat top of the cabin roof. When seated, the pilot's head was about in line with the bottom wing and the view out through angular boat-like windows was onto a flat deck-like nose in which there was a round hatch, through which crew could emerge to throw out an anchor or wield a boat hook. The tailplane was mounted three-quarters of the way up the fin in the full blow of the propeller, which made the aircraft very sensitive to elevator and rudder control, especially at full throttle. On the ground it waddled along like a duck, on relatively large wheels which, for some reason, we were asked never to retract unless landing on water – which under normal circumstances we were not allowed to do. Undercarriage retraction, which was by hand-pump, was pretty unimportant as it was only said to raise cruising speed from 85 to 87 knots.

The undercarriage warning horn sounded whenever the throttle was closed, irrespective of whether the undercarriage was up or down. This, in theory, was to remind the pilot that the undercarriage was in the correct position, 'up' for landing on water and 'down' for an airfield landing. This warning arrangement no doubt contributed, despite the advice not to raise the undercarriage, to the incidences of wheels-up landings. If landed on grass there was sometimes no damage to either float or hull, the prop being well clear of the ground. On the ground the Walrus tended to weathercock and was nose heavy. In a crosswind therefore it was necessary to taxi very carefully as it was all too easy to touch the ground with a float and damage it. As one trundled over the ground for take-off the Walrus would make small darts to left or right and when finally one pulled the stick back to get airborne, it climbed away swinging gently from left to right in pendulous motion. Certainly there was no other aircraft like it! The Walrus was later replaced by the Sea Otter, a similar aircraft but with a conventional tractor propeller which, being in front of the wings, was unpleasantly near the pilot's head, a change that made the aircraft even more nose-heavy.

In the New Year all but three of the male members of the Ferry Pool were posted and the women were left to run the Pool on their own. The previous head of the Pool, Australian Geoff Wikner, had left

Charles Dutton, a one-armed pilot employed by the ATA who is recorded as having ferried 541 Spitfires.

when we arrived. He was the pre-war designer of the two-seater Wicko, one of which I bought and flew in a number of air races after the war when I was at Boscombe Down. Later, in peacetime, he hit the headlines when, with sea passages impossible to come by, he bought and converted for civil flying an old Halifax in which he flew himself, his family and some fare-paying passengers back to Australia.

Of the three pilots who remained, one was Bruce Campbell, who later left ATA to become a test pilot with de Havilland. Another was George Dutton whose brother Charles, a one-armed ferry pilot, remained in ATA

Armstrong Payn

until it closed by which time he had ferried 541 Spitfires and 279 Tempests and Typhoons. The third to remain was Armstrong Payn, whose brother Murray Payn had taught Prince Bernard to fly at Hatfield and with whom I remained in touch until he died shortly afterwards. As well as Spitfires and Oxfords there was the occasional Blenheim to be collected from the Cunliffe Owen factory at Southampton. Women had to be cleared to fly the Blenheim before the men left, thus about a month after arriving at Hamble I found myself being sent to White Waltham where pilots for ATA's Class 4 were cleared on an ATA school Blenheim. Pilots so cleared could fly not only Blenheims, but also other twin-engined bombers such as the Whitley, Hampden or even the Wellington without further instruction. The only twin calling for further clearance was the Hudson, for which I took a separate course later. My instructor on the Blenheim course was BOAC Captain Griffiths who, after 2 hours and 15 minutes dual, sent me off on 2 hours and 20 minutes solo, after which I returned to Hamble to ferry the occasional Blenheim. When I arrived at Hamble the only operational aircraft I had flown were eight Hurricanes and two Spitfires, and yet by October we had been cleared to fly, as well as single-engined types such as the Walrus and Tomahawk, the Blenheim and the Hampden. By the end of October there were at Hamble, some eight pilots qualified to fly the very limited number of operational twins that came their way.

CHAPTER 12

NO. 6 FERRY POOL, RATCLIFFE

I had only been at Hamble for some six weeks when a further move came up which extended the role of women pilots. When the ferrying of operational aircraft was thrown open to women on an equal basis to the men, there was a backlog of women capable of qualifying to fly operational twin-engined types because they had been held back for so long. At Hamble there were now eight pilots, including the three men, who had done the Blenheim course and were qualified for flying the very limited number of operational twins that came the way of the Hamble Ferry Pool. Yet meanwhile, in some of the all-male Pools, with the Halifax and Stirling coming into large scale production and numbers of ATA male pilots qualifying to fly them, there was an increasing call for women pilots to ferry the larger twins.

These were the circumstances under which a few women were asked to volunteer for posting to No. 6 Ferry Pool at Ratcliffe, a previously all-male Pool. Ratcliffe, once the private landing ground of Sir Lindsay Everard MP, was situated on the Fosse Way some eight miles north of Leicester and I was one of a group of four who volunteered to go there. Two of us, Ruth Lambton and myself, were from Hamble, while Gabby Patterson and Ursula Preston were from Hatfield, and we reported there on 16th November 1941. For me it was the start of the only two months that I could possibly term as 'unhappy' during my whole time in ATA.

My memories of Ratcliffe, if few, are vivid. In ATA generally, pilots gravitated to Ferry Pools which suited them both flying-wise and socially. No. 6 pool had collected together a band of relatively young, tough and self-assured pilots, many of them Americans, who had much more flying experience than us and liked to think of themselves as dead-end kids who could deliver their aircraft when even the birds were walking. This I found intimidating and quite different from the sort of pilots I had so far worked with. As to the work, the pool was associated

Defiants were collected from the Boulton & Paul factory at Wolverhampton.

with a wide variety of Midland wartime aircraft factories, first and fore-most of which was the Vickers factory at Castle Bromwich with its large output of Spitfires. Although women had only recently qualified to fly them, this could have been why the women had been posted there. Other factories included Standard Motors at Ansty, from where we collected Oxfords – something again which the women were acquainted with – and the Boulton & Paul factory at Wolverhampton, from where Defiants were collected. We had been sent to Ratcliffe in the short days of winter, at the worst possible time as regards weather and, coming from the south, we were unfamiliar with the Midlands and the smog-laden air which resulted from the factories. This was at a time when coal was the only fuel available for heating both factories and homes, and the belching smoke gave rise to perpetually bad visibility in winter. With anticyclonic conditions and an inversion, smoke could hang around for days on end, turning haze into fog which, as map-reading was our only means of navigation, made finding one's way in the air difficult at the best of times. Above the smog, cloud would form, adding to the prob-lems. Down south, even at Hatfield, there had been at that time no large-scale industrial development to deal with and so we had not had to cope with a perpetually smoke-filled atmosphere. Ratcliffe, it can be said in retrospect, was in fact no place for newly qualified pilots to be posted for the first time in winter! A south-west wind would bring the Birmingham smoke to Leicester and, for much of the winter, the area from Birmingham to Leicester and from Derby to the Potteries was an area of continuous poor visibility. Sometimes when sun and blue skies stretched over the blanket of fog, the Birmingham balloons would be let up until they broke through the murk, shining like silver in the sunshine. For once they provided a useful navigation aid; but getting out of sight of the ground was not encouraged as getting back could present serious problems. In any case 'flying over the top' was strictly against ATA rules, although out of sheer necessity it was sometimes done. To navigate oneself round this area in poor visibility one needed to know every detail of the surrounding countryside so that a fleeting glance of road, railway or factory below could pinpoint exactly where one was in relation to airfields and more importantly, to the balloons.

If it were possible to wear a groove in the sky there must surely have been one over the Fosse Way, passing as it did the boundary of Ratcliffe airfield. It could be followed continuously over roads, through fields or even woods by pilots going to and returning from the much used Maintenance Units of Little Rissington, Kemble and Aston Down. North of Ratcliffe where the Fosse Way had become a main road, it could be even more dependently followed when delivering aircraft to the north, ensuring that one was clear of the Nottingham balloons.

For the first two days after we arrived there was no flying. On the third day I was given a Hurricane to take from Rearsby to Kirkbride with a Blenheim back to Watton. This was the day on which 'Wally' Handley, well-known pre-war racing motor cyclist and now Commanding Office of No. 3 Ferry Pool at Hawarden, took off in an Airacobra – a single-seat American aircraft which had recently gone into

Bell P-39 Airacobra

limited service with the RAF. On take-off the engine was heard to be over-revving with smoke pouring from it. There was then an explosion and the aircraft dived into the ground; this was the second loss of an ATA senior officer.

Two more days of 'no flying' followed and our Commanding Officer was being pressed from the highest level to clear the Spitfires which were building up at the Castle Bromwich factory awaiting dispatch. This, the largest Spitfire factory in the country, was on the outskirts of Birmingham and was surrounded on three sides by balloons for its defence. The balloons stretched to the western side of the airstrip so all take-offs had to be made to the east, and the ATA taxi Ansons that

The Castle Bromwich Aircraft Factory.

brought us in had, regardless of wind, to land to the west, turn round and take off in the opposite direction. And so it was that, some four days after our arrival, a group which included all four of the women were piled into an Anson for delivery to Castle Bromwich. The weather, even for the Anson, was distinctly borderline to the extent that at the first attempt the senior and very experienced Anson pilot turned back. At 4 o'clock however the urgency was such that he was told to have another go on this November evening at getting there. This time he managed to make it and we – who had never been to Castle Bromwich before and so did not know the lie of the country – were disgorged clutching our ferry chits. As the weather was bad, we were to take our Spitfires only as far as Ratcliffe. Gabby and Ruth very sensibly decided not to start. Ursula and I however, said we would have a go with the men who, having done this trip many times before, were familiar with the surrounding country. For me this was one of my most unpleasant flights of the many I made in ATA. Cloud was low and visibility poor and the Spitfire was not the easiest of aircraft to see the ground from in these conditions. I was not familiar with the landmarks and, with little time before darkness fell on this winter's evening, the chance of making a safe landing would have been unlikely if one got lost. As it was, I managed to follow the railway to Nuneaton and even that wasn't easy because it turned north, then south but, somehow, I managed to stick with it until I picked up the Fosse Way which I followed to Ratcliffe.

In the event all of us including Ursula managed to arrive safely, but I still felt that we should not have been sent out on our first trips from Castle Bromwich in those conditions, and said so. But back at the Ferry Pool, not knowing about the urgent necessity to move the aircraft, I got a black mark for complaining and until the end of the month was confined to flying Oxfords and the Puss Moth taxi. I have often wondered since then whether Ursula Preston was as shattered by the trip as I was. One didn't normally discuss such things out of reluctance no doubt to admit to others who were apparently radiating confidence, that one had frightened oneself. Also, once back safely on the ground, problems were quickly forgotten and replaced by satisfaction that one had, nevertheless, managed to complete a difficult delivery.

But this episode had done nothing to alleviate my general disenchantment with No. 6 Ferry Pool. This was not helped by my living conditions. Ruth, who had been married and had already shared a flat with Ursula at Hatfield, was more organised domestically and probably financially, and had again taken a flat with Ursula. I, however, had never cooked or catered for myself and in wartime with food rationing it was not an easy time to start. Not a great one for 'digs' or being committed to warning my landlady every time I was going to be out for a meal or for the night, I plumped for the Bell Hotel in Leicester where if you were away for more than a couple of nights, you had to hand your ration

*Handley Page
Hampden*

book to the hotel. This fed and housed me reasonably but offered nothing for the evening or free time. After the friendliness of both Hatfield and Hamble, I found the long winter evenings of wartime England both lonely and depressing. Living in a Midland town was definitely a mistake, at least for me! After this life went on with a preponderance of Oxfords and Spits and the occasional Defiant out of Wolverhampton. However we had been sent to No. 6 Ferry Pool as Class 4 pilots, which entitled us to fly Hampdens and Wellingtons, although few came on the books. My requests to fly one of the latter was met with little enthusiasm, but after much nagging I finally got a Hampden. In fact during that week I got four, all from No. 8 Maintenance Unit at Little Rissington to Addington for No. 44 Squadron Cottesmore. The Hampden with its two 1,000 hp Bristol Pegasus engines was a great improvement on the Hereford of which, gratefully, I flew only one. The Hereford was generally similar to the Hampden but had Napier Dagger engines of which, with their unusual configuration of twin crankshafts geared to drive a single airscrew, we had every reason to be suspicious.

Thus November turned into December and finally December went out with a burst of 'no flying'. Two days before Christmas I acquired my first chit for a Wellington, but bad weather prevented the

Blackburn Botha

movement. But I did not seem to fit in at Ratcliffe. I had even contemplated leaving ATA altogether and had been down to London where, over lunch at Claridges, I had discussed the possibility of joining Fred and Blossom Miles at their factory at Woodley. Gabby Patterson was also unhappy with the new Ferry Pool, but Ruth and Ursula were both settling in, having decided that any 'mixed' Ferry Pool was better than the cloistered life of either Hatfield or Hamble. Ruth, whose RAF husband had already been killed in the war, later married American ATA pilot Eddy Ballard. Ursula eventually married Richard Metcalfe, a member of the Ratcliffe Operations Staff, and faded from ATA. Before this she survived a serious accident resulting from an engine failure in a Botha, not one of our favourite aircraft. I too much preferred the mixed environment but if one all-male Ferry Pool were to take female ferry pilots, why not another? My sights were already set on No. 1 Ferry Pool at White Waltham. But, when in early January 1942 I was posted back to Hatfield, it was like returning home.

CHAPTER 13

RETURN TO HATFIELD

The Hatfield I returned to was a very different one from the one I had left less than nine months before. Most of my contemporaries had gone to Hamble and the Pool now consisted of the somewhat older original eight, less Rosemary Rees who had gone to Hamble, plus a large contingent of later joiners who flew Hurricanes and Spitfires but not as yet twin-engined types. Joan Hughes and Margaret Cunnison were still doing a certain amount of instruction and Margie Fairweather and Winnie Crossley spent most of their time flying the taxi Anson. This left me in a fairly strong position as regards any twin-engined aircraft that might came our way for ferrying. Pauline Gower, who was now chiefly concerned with the recruitment of new women pilots, had joined the ATA headquarters' staff at White Waltham and her place as Commanding Officer of No.5 Ferry Pool had been taken by Marion Wilberforce, with Winnie Crossley her second in command.

Flying apart, after the aloneness of Leicester it was grand to be back with people one could go for walks with, or to the cinema, play squash with on the de Havilland airfield squash court or, when there was no flying, lunch at The Comet. This wasn't just other members of the ATA; we had friends amongst the de Havilland test pilots, the RAFVR flying school instructors and others who worked on or near the airfield. There was never a reason to be on one's own unless it was by choice. Whenever I found myself with a couple of days off I still went back to Hamble, from where the male pilots had not as yet been posted. It was relatively easy to find an aircraft that needed ferrying in that direction and for getting back I could normally get an Oxford or a Walrus to White Waltham, though once when the weather was impossible I had to catch a cold and slow train to Reading.

January and February of 1942 produced the usual quota of snow and non-flying weather. When we did manage to get an aircraft to its correct destination something invariably happened to the 'taxi' programme so that one ended up spending the night either away from base or in a train. de Havillands had ceased to turn out Oxfords from Hatfield but were still producing the odd Rapide, or Dominie as the military version was called. These too, more often than not, went up north. It was a Dominie that I took to Dumfries in early February to collect my first Wellington.

The Wellington was, as far as ATA was concerned, classed with the Blenheim and the Hampden, so before flying it was simply a question of reading the Pilots' Notes. Of all the steps forward we took without training, this to me was the biggest. We had done a brief course on the Blenheim, which weighed less than 14,000 lb and had a wingspan of some forty-two feet. The Wellington weighed some 24,000 lb, had a wingspan of eighty-six or so feet, felt much heavier and had far more sluggish controls than the smaller twins. The ATA flying school was shortly to change over from Blenheims to Wellingtons for Class 4 training. The Wellington, as is now well known, was of geodetic basket-weave construction, a type of structure derived from design studies made by Barnes Wallis for the Airship R100. This made it very flexible and when the ailerons were operated the aircraft flexed so that in gusty

Vickers-Armstrong Wellington

weather you could see the wingtips moving up and down. To counter the large trim change which occurred when the flaps were lowered, the flaps were connected mechanically to the trimming mechanism. Thus, when the flaps were lowered, nose-down trim was automatically applied and the trimmer wheel turned appropriately without pilot action. There was, however, a snag to this. If the trimmer wheel was already set forward of neutral when the flaps were lowered, nose-down trim was automatically applied and the elevator trim tab, already partly raised, would reach its full 'up' travel before the flaps were fully down. The continued movement of the flaps could seriously strain or, at the worst, break the elevator trim cables.

In ATA you were invariably deemed 'lucky' when you were given a ferry chit for a type of aircraft you had not flown before. I however worried quite a bit when confronted for the first time with something as large and different as the Wellington. The one I collected from No. 18 Maintenance Unit at Dumfries on Friday, February 13th, was a relatively docile 'Peggy,' a Bristol-built Mk I powered by Pegasus engines. There were many varieties of Wellington and no less than four different makes of engines were fitted.

The Mk.III, which entered service in 1942, had Hercules engines and was the mainstay of the bomber fleet until four-engined bombers arrived. One of the projects they were used for it is recorded, consisted of towing Spitfires from Gibraltar to within range of Malta where they would be released. Whilst being towed, however, the Spitfire propellers windmilled, fouling up the plugs and leaving the pilots with dead-stick landings at Malta. The Mk.IV had twin Wasp engines and the Mk.II Merlins. Different marks of Wellingtons had many minor differences for the pilot. Some, for example, had red lights to show that the undercarriage was retracted, on others they indicated that it was in transit. Wellingtons destined for Coastal Command had airspeed indicators in knots – an unusual feature for those days. One such version had 'Christmas Tree' aerials for detecting submarines and another had a huge de-gaussing ring circling the whole aircraft horizontally which was used for exploding magnetic mines. Wellingtons could also be fitted with air-surface-vessel (ASV) radar and with Leigh searchlights. There was even a Mark VI pressurised version designed for high altitude work in

which partial pressurisation had been achieved by lining the forward end of the fuselage with what amounted to a vast steel boiler. In this model there was also a shallow Perspex dome above the pilot's seat though which there was virtually no downward view, which made taxiing particularly difficult. Rejected by the Pathfinders, ATA had the task of ferrying these from factory to Maintenance Units where they were broken up for spares. Ferrying this unpleasant aircraft was reserved for the most experienced pilots and happily I was never given one! A White Waltham pilot was ferrying one when the dome blew off, leaving his unprotected head sticking out of the top of the aeroplane in the full slipstream. The Wellington VI was one of the aircraft never listed in ATA's Pilots' Notes. In all its guises it must have been the largest twin-engined aircraft that ATA pilots flew solo.

The pressurised Wellington Mk VI.

But at Hatfield the days of the Ferry Pool were numbered. The Mosquito, which had first flown in 1940, was now coming off the production line and de Havillands, who had never been great defenders of the ATA cause, were anxious to get rid of their ever-expanding lodger unit. In April 1942, therefore, No. 5 Ferry Pilots' Pool moved from Hatfield to Luton. Here ATA's new Elementary Flying Training School (EFTS) was being set up to train pilots with no previous flying experience who were now being taken on. The 'older' pilots from Hatfield were sent there to help out with the newcomers and Margaret Cunnison and Joan Hughes went there to instruct in the EFTS. The light aircraft of the cross-country flight, which were getting in the way of the larger training types at White Waltham, were also moved to Luton and American women pilots who were just starting to arrive were sent there to be familiarised with UK wartime flying conditions. The new No.5 Ferry Pool was planned from the start as a 'mixed' pool i.e. for training both sexes; it was to provide the training of pilots ab initio through all necessary stages until they could fly Spitfires. The move from White Waltham of ATA's light aircraft and the cross-country flight, involved the transfer of some ten flying instructors, 69 aircraft and 75 engineers to cope with the maintenance of both school and ferry aircraft.

'Frankie' Francis off duty at White Waltham.

The few remaining and mostly more recently-joined pilots still at Hatfield were sent for the most part to join the new all-woman Ferry Pool at Hamble. So far, Ratcliffe had been the only Ferry Pool to accept women pilots – a matter left to the relevant Pool Commanding Officer to decide. At White Waltham, No. 1 Ferry Pool was headed by Francis Francis, millionaire, ex-Guards Officer and pre-war private aircraft owner, who had reached international standards at golf. Slight and dark with very blue eyes, he was a born leader, espe-cially good at dealing with the roughs and toughs in his Pool, with whom he generally got on better than with the bosses 'upstairs'. All the girls he met fell for him and I was no exception. One must assume that by opting out of both Hamble and then Ratcliffe I was being labelled, 'difficult to place'. Luton would have not been my scene as I preferred flying to looking after newcomers, so the only alternative seemed for me to go back to Hamble, where I don't think I would have been wanted anyway.

Fortunately, although Frankie was not prepared to make his Ferry Pool a mixed pool, the challenge of taking on someone with a reputation for being 'difficult' would, I am sure, have been a challenge he could not resist. He agreed to accept me into his Ferry Pool, but with a stern warning that I could expect no special treatment and, work wise, would have to slot in on an equal basis with the men.

Almost my last ferry trip before leaving Hatfield was a Percival Q.6 from Broxbourne to the Royal Navy at Lee-on-Solent. The aircraft had an early variety of the electrically-operated variable pitch Ratier propeller. In 1942 one still had to land at the RN station at Worthy Down to get clearance for entering the defended south coast area. After

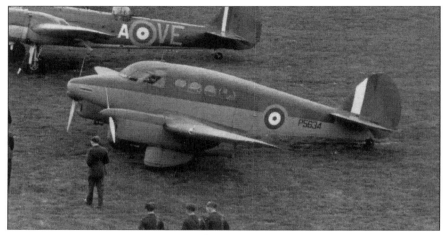

Percival Q.6.

take-off I had reduced rpm in the usual manner but when I came to land at Worthy Down I was unable to increase them again; the more I tried to increase them the lower they sank. I tried to explain my problem to a naval rating, but he knew no more about Ratier propellers than I did. Since leaving an aircraft anywhere other than at its correct destination was apt to cause problems, I decided that, revs or no revs, I would press on to Lee. Here, in spite of a rather short runway, I handed over the aircraft in one piece to the Royal Navy where it was planned to be used as a communications aircraft. After the war Duncan Hamilton, of motor racing fame, who was in the Navy at Lee-on-Solent at the time, told me that this aircraft had been allotted there for his personal use. I never found the reason for the propeller problem but, in retrospect, I believe it may simply have been due to a flat battery.

From Hatfield I first went to the AFTS at White Waltham to be checked out on the Hudson, enabling me to join the select band of three or four women from Hamble who were already cleared to fly all types of

*Lockheed
Hudson*

twin-engined aircraft. The Hudson was never one of my favourite aircraft; it was what we called a 'swinger,' meaning that it had a marked tendency to swing during the landing run. We were expected, as with all other types of aircraft, to 'three-point' it, that is to touch down with main and tail wheels at the same time. This involved a marked change of attitude during 'flare out,' which reduced the effectiveness of the rudder during the landing run. The other thing that took a bit of getting used to was the brakes, which were operated by pulling a car-type ratchet lever set in the central pedestal to the right of the pilot's seat. In order therefore to produce differential braking through rudder bar movement, one had theoretically to set the lever a couple of notches out, a setting difficult to find. Thus if braking was called for during the landing run one had to lean to one side and pull, making sure that at the same time the rudder bar was correctly operated. If during this manoeuvre differential brake was unwittingly applied, the landing run could end in a ground loop, as was not uncommonly demonstrated. Luckily the Hudson undercarriage was robust and the pilot usually got away with it. This was just as well as the fuel tanks were directly above the undercarriage struts and a heavy landing could lead to ruptured fuel tanks and fire.

Having been cleared for the Hudson I was seconded on a temporary basis to No. 1 Ferry Pool where I got involved in the rush of priority Spitfires to Scotland. On 24th April, at the personal request of

Churchill, Roosevelt had agreed to the loan of the United States aircraft carrier *Wasp* to deliver Spitfires to Malta. *Wasp* had already delivered 47 Spitfires, but the Germans had seen them arrive and had made them their special target. The state of Malta at this time was critical, so Churchill turned again to Roosevelt to allow *Wasp* to make one more trip. This was agreed and on May 1st 64 Spitfires were loaded on *Wasp* in the Clyde and she again set sail for Malta

This then is where ATA again came into the story. As *Wasp* couldn't hang about in the Clyde, the aircraft had to be delivered with the utmost urgency to Renfrew. All ferry chits involved in these very special movements were printed in red and marked 'P.1.W,' which stood for 'Priority 1, WAIT.' The significance of the 'W' was that, in order to be ready to take the aircraft away from Maintenance Units where their final equipment was fitted, pilots had to be sent out to collect them before the aircraft was signalled as ready. In some cases this meant staying overnight in order to be available the moment the aircraft was pushed out. If the aircraft took longer than expected to be cleared, or there was a last-minute snag, the pilot had to stay with it until either this had been rectified or the aircraft had been replaced.

A Spitfire similar to those delivered to the Wasp.

Curtiss P-40 Tomahawk

In this second rush, I took part with others from White Waltham in the delivery of Spitfires – in my case from Brize Norton to Prestwick. After delivering one on April 27th the shortage of pilots for this trip was such that we were flown back to White Waltham in a Rapide, a journey of three hours and forty minutes! The following day, after delivering a Hurricane from Langley to Cardiff and a Spitfire from Llandow to Duxford, I was again sent out to Colerne to take a Spitfire to Prestwick, arriving there a 9.25 pm. On a clear spring evening this had been a glorious trip. I also see from my log book that I flew at this time both my first Kittyhawk and my first Tomahawk. I have particular memories of the Tomahawk which I took from Wroughton to Oxford (Kidlington) because it was one taken over from a batch ordered by the French on which the throttle opened in the opposite direction to normal, i.e. it had to be moved forward to close it and pulled backward to open it. On the approach I remember concentrating as never before as, if more power was called for, one had to remember not to do what was usual, push the throttle forward!

CHAPTER 14

SPRING 1942: BACK TO HAMBLE

In early May I was posted to Hamble for three weeks where, I can only assume, they were temporarily short of pilots. The scope of the Hamble Ferry Pool had widened considerably since I was there some six months previously and whilst there I flew two types of aircraft I hadn't flown before, the Beaufort and the Airacobra. Throughout the war certain aircraft would appear on ATA's books and then, luckily in some cases, disappear as suddenly as they had come. The Airacobra was one such aircraft.

The Bell Airacobra was a highly unorthodox single-seat fighter. Its Allison engine was mounted behind the cockpit, a ten-foot shaft which passed under the pilot's seat connecting it with a Curtis electric propeller. This arrangement made it possible for the nose to be fitted with a cannon and heavy machine guns synchronised to fire through the propeller. The engine, which was on the centre of gravity would, it was thought, give greater manoeuvrability and the nose-wheel provide the pilot with greater visibility than with tail-wheel fighters. Six hundred of these aircraft had been ordered by the RAF, and in 1941 three went to the Fighter Development Unit at Duxford for evaluation. Its performance was found to be disappointing; the take-off run of 750 yards was considered unacceptably long and during trials by No. 601 Squadron, modifications and lack of spares contributed to a high rate of unserviceability. In December 1941 it was withdrawn from the RAF and of the 600 or so ordered 200 were diverted to Russia. Others were taken over by the Australian Air Force for use in the Pacific and a few went to the Free French.

Airacobras arrived at Southampton Docks in crates and were assembled by Cunliffe Owen at Eastleigh. An article in The Aeroplane ran: "The Airacobra has all the disadvantages of both pusher and tractor (propeller) layouts, with some more of its own." The handling notes also make interesting reading. "At idling speed," the notes ran, "the whole aeroplane shakes violently. As a result the engine should not be run on

*A Bell P-39
Airacobra in
service with 601
Squadron*

the ground at less than 1,000 rpm except when landing (to keep the landing run within reasonable length), and momentarily when necessary for manoeuvring. Roughness is also evident in flight but seems least at about 1,800 rpm." The pitot-head was mounted on a 30 in pole which protruded from the leading edge of the port wing. In flight a good guide, the notes continued, is to watch the pitot-head shaft which reacts to vibration in a lively manner. For cruise, ATA pilots were advised to select rpm for minimum vibration. One of the more worrying features was the unreliability of the pop-up nosewheel 'down' indicator as rumour had it that if the nose wheel collapsed on landing, the engine would come forward, hitting the pilot in the back!

Entry to the cockpit was by means of a large car-type door, complete with adjustable glass windows. "Owing to their light construction," the notes read, "the doors are rather flexible. It is therefore ESSENTIAL TO WIND THE WINDOWS RIGHT DOWN before slamming the doors shut or the windows may be broken by cracking." The electric undercarriage and flap operating switch could be selected 'electric' or 'manual'. When the latter was set the undercarriage wound down by handle. Pilots were warned, however, that if 'manual' was set for normal operation, the winding handle driven by the motor presented a serious risk of injuring the pilot. With the cancellation of the RAF contract the women pilots at Hamble got more than their fair share of the job moving these aircraft from Marwell, the Cunliffe Owen satellite outside the balloons, to Maintenance Units where they went back into crates for delivery overseas.

When a new type came onto ATA's books, senior staff from White Waltham would if chance arose take the opportunity to fly one. It was while I was at Hamble that Philip Wills, ATA's Chief Operations Officer, decided to try his hand at the Airacobra, so for his convenience a Cunliffe Owen test pilot brought one to Hamble for him. Any of us that were around at the time went out to watch the take-off. The Airacobra was noted for its long take-off run so those watching were horrified to see him Philip line up for take-off on Hamble's short easterly run. Without radio there was nothing that could be done to stop him. So we watched, mesmerised, as the aircraft hurtled across the grass airfield and rose in the air just in time to cross the fence. It then sank down out of sight towards the river bed. The test pilot, who was watching with us, said in an unemotional tone, "Well, that's the end of your C.O.O." Luckily, seconds later, the aircraft reappeared, climbed away and set course for its destination.

As previously mentioned, Walter 'Wally' Handley, Commanding Officer of ATA's No. 3 Ferry Pool at Hawarden, was a pre-war motorcycle and Isle of Man Tourist Trophy rider who had survived a number of horrendous crashes but was killed in an Airacobra. He had picked up the aircraft from Kirkbride for delivery to Hawarden. Shortly after take-off the engine was heard to be over-revving with black smoke coming out of the exhaust. This was followed by an explosion, after which it crashed. Take-off boost, unlike that on British engines, had to be set for take-off at 2,800 rpm maximum and over-boosting was suggested as the most likely cause. Wally, or 'Handlebars' as he was known by his pilots, had, as his obituary said, "forfeited his ninth life and passed from this troublesome world to a more peaceful sphere."

It was in an Oxford from Portsmouth that I returned on 23rd of May to White Waltham after my detachment to Hamble. The digs I had been living in near White Waltham, had a goldfish pond that had been emptied for repair and needed replenishing. On Portsmouth airfield there was an enormous lily pond where goldfish had grown to the size of herrings. The Air Inspection Department happened to have in their office a fishing net and, with this and a jam jar, we went out to the pool to see what we could catch. I had caught about three with the borrowed net – which was not easy as the pool was large enough for them to escape into the middle – when some brown-coated members of the airfield defence appeared. The airfield, they said, had been requisitioned and the requisition included both the pond and the fish. After losing a verbal battle I had therefore to give up with the few I had already caught, so returned to collect my paperwork and sign up for my aircraft. There was nowhere in it to put the jam jar (which had no lid), so I rested it as best I could on the adjoining seat where I could take hold of it if it looked like spilling its contents – which it did most of the time. Still, they arrived at their destination somehow and were put to swim in the much smaller Berkshire pond where they survived, at least for a time. My new digs were in Littlewick Green, only a few miles from the airfield. The house was owned by Mrs Miller whose two daughters who had been at Benenden School with me.

CHAPTER 15

No. 1 FERRY POOL, WHITE WALTHAM

This then was the start of my time with No. 1 Ferry Pool White Waltham, some of the most fulfilling months of my life. At Hatfield, because of the relatively few types of aircraft we were allowed to fly, work had been strictly limited and we had to take it in turns for the more interesting jobs. Frequently we were unable to fly at all, simply because there was nothing on our books to be moved. At Hamble there was plenty of work but the trips were short and one could do several in one day, but there was a lot of hanging about in between them and, as far as types were concerned, there was an over-abundance of Spitfires and Oxfords and we still had to take it in turns for the more interesting types.

At White Waltham there was all the flying one could wish for and a wider range of aircraft to fly. The skills of the male pilots there also varied enormously, from the staid, older ex-airline types to the young and exuberant who, for one reason or another – eyesight being a typical example – had not been accepted into the Services. There were also some young Americans. From all these, in their different ways, there was much to be learnt and for me, the variety and healthy competition that came from the mixture of skills and individuals was wholly stimulating. The area over which the Ferry Pool operated was also much larger, extending from the south coast to Prestwick, from Manston to St. David's Head and to Norfolk, Lincolnshire and Yorkshire.

The challenge for me was to keep my end up with the rest of the Pool flying-wise. The only other woman pilot at White Waltham when I joined was Margie Fairweather; she had been one of the first women pilots to join the women's Ferry Pool at Hatfield in January 1940. When the second intake – of which I was one – was taken on in the summer of 1940, she reverted to ferrying us around in the taxi Anson. But before Hatfield closed in April 1942, she had joined her husband Douglas at Prestwick where for a short time, he had been Deputy Pool Commander. When he was moved to White Waltham soon after to take charge of 'Air

PILOTS | CLASS | LEAVE | POSITION | LAST SIGNAL | DATE | PILOTS | CLASS | LEAVE | POSITION | LAST SIGNAL | DATE | EV ENGINEER | CLA

The censored Ops Board at White Waltham

Movements', a name given to a newly-formed ATA Communications Flight, Margie joined him. It was whilst flying for Air Movements that in August 1944, she was killed when making a forced landing after engine failure in a Percival Proctor when the aircraft, which had a fixed under-carriage, ran into a ditch. Her two passengers were only slightly injured.

ATA's headquarters and hangar at White Waltham had been purpose-built for the Flying Training School set up by de Havillands in 1935, which was forced out by ATA at the end of 1940. ATA's Operations Room, which must have been designed for a similar purpose, was glazed on three sides. Two sides overlooked the tarmac outside the hangar and the airfield, and the third the main corridor which led from the building to the tarmac past the parachute store. In ATA's time the Operations Room was manned by the Pool's Operations Officers who, under the direction of the Pool C.O. in an adjacent office, made out the ferry chits which were doled out each day to pilots, specifying their task or tasks. These chits were laid out by the operations staff on a long polished shelf adjacent to the Operations Room. It was here that we came when we arrived at nine o'clock in the morning to see what the day had in store for us. If the chits were not yet out we would go over to the Mess alongside the main building or wait in a rest room. The remaining side of the Ops. Room was covered by a large blackboard, which showed the names of the Pool's pilots, their category indicating the types of aircraft each was cleared to fly, and whether they were available for flight, were sick or on leave.

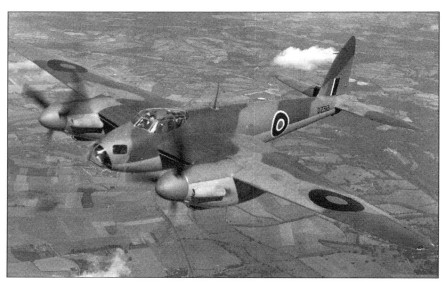

*de Havilland
Mosquito*

Within a week of joining No. 1 Ferry Pool I had flown two new aircraft types, the Beaufighter and the Mosquito. I was given the Beaufighter, a Mk. I with Hercules engines, on my first day with the Pool. It came on the books in the late afternoon as a 'priority' task and was given to me because there was no one else available. It had to go from St. Athan to 30 MU, Little Sealand. Five days later I was given a chit for a Mk. II Mosquito from Hatfield to St. Athan, and from there I had a Hurricane to Shoreham. Of the two high-performance twins I tended to prefer the Beaufighter although this was not the popular choice. I liked the roomy cockpit with its centrally-placed seat, the rugged trimmers and throttle levers and its solid wide-spaced undercarriage. It was currently rumored that if on take-off at full power an engine failed before a speed of 160 mph had been reached, the resulting roll could not be controlled. Hence the aircraft was termed a 'killer' – but for one reason or another this could be said of several other twins. The most unusual feature of the Beaufighter was the pilot's emergency exit. The main entrance hatch – which was also the emergency exit – was on the bottom of the fuselage aft of the pilot's seat. To reach his seat after climbing through the hatch the pilot had then to climb over the back of the seat, which was designed to collapse backwards into a horizontal position to make this possible. Two handrails in the roof were provided for the pilots to hold on to whilst – as the Notes said: 'the pilot swung his legs over the back of the seat' and in fact, this must have been the only

Bristol Beaufighter

aircraft for which Handling Notes devoted the best part of a page to describing how the pilot got in and out of the cockpit. It must surely have been about this aircraft that Boscombe Down is alleged to have written: 'Entry into this aircraft is difficult; it is recommended that it is made impossible!'

In order to leave the aircraft, the pilot had once more to collapse the back of the seat and, should he need to vacate the aircraft in the air, pull a wire lanyard to unlock the entrance hatch. I have never met anyone who did this but, every now and then, pilots would come back with hair-raising stories of how the back of the seat collapsed, usually when they were landing. This led to specific instructions to check before take-off that the back of the seat was properly locked!

The popularity of the Mosquito with ATA pilots came generally from its speed, manoeuvrability and good single-engine performance but, like most things in life, it also had its less favourable points. The cockpit was cramped and somewhat claustrophobic. One climbed in using a flimsy, portable ladder through a relatively small hatch on the port side or in the bomber version, in the bottom of the cockpit floor. The cockpit had two side-by-side seats which were staggered so as to make room for them; there was no room for a control pedestal. The throttle box was hard against the curved side of the fuselage and the throttles had to be opened with the fingers rather than with the palm of the hand. Only 12 lb of boost was allowed to be used for take-off and, because of the marked tendency to swing to port, ATA Pilots' Notes recommended that not more than 2 lb boost should be applied – obtained with less than quarter throttle – until at least one third of the take-off run had been completed. The take-off safety speed was given as 170 mph and when on full load the Mosquito had more than its fair share of take-off accidents. Although clean and drag-free in the air it called for a great deal of power once undercarriage and flaps were down and, even lightly loaded as ATA flew it, the recommended over-the-hedge speed of 125 mph when landing was high for aircraft of that era.

Not only were ferry trips themselves now longer, but taxi rides were longer too with many more stops increasing the length of a day's work. During May and June that year I spent more hours in the air and ferried more aircraft than at any time since joining ATA. As a newcomer I only flew the taxi Ansons occasionally and then when they were lightly loaded. Because it could involve the safety of up to ten other pilots this job was reserved for senior members of the Pool and for one or two older, and less active, pilots of proven flying ability for whom a day spent sitting in an Anson entailed less physical and mental stress than climbing in and out of less forgiving aircraft.

As a means of gaining experience, pilots still under training were used for Fairchild taxi work but flew the aircraft only when there were no passengers. So when a 'stooge' pilot picked up a ferry pilot, he

Karpeles-Schenker and Martin Steynor in one of the taxi Ansons.

*onnie Malcolm
ho, on account
his portly
ature, confined
imself to taxi
ilot duties on
nsons.*

or she handed over the controls. Even between ferry pilots there was an unwritten code of etiquette whereby, if one picked up a more senior pilot in a taxi aircraft, one offered to hand over the controls. The days I enjoyed best were ones when I was free from taxi aircraft and could work at my own pace. Inevitably the pace at which pilots worked varied widely. Some stopped for lunch whenever they got the chance, even if this involved getting transport to an RAF Mess or holding up a taxi aircraft. Others, like myself, preferred to fly first and eat afterwards. As a result I tended to be given the longer and what we thought of as the more interesting jobs.

"We've given you these because we thought you would enjoy them," I remember Frankie saying to me one day when I collected ferry chits for a Wellington from Brooklands to St. Athan, a Beaufighter from St. Athan to Dumfries and an elderly Battle from Dumfries to Odiham – and of course I did!

For those who didn't take time off to go to a Mess there was usually a cup of tea and a roll to be had from a small on-site canteen provided at Maintenance Units for men working on the aircraft. For some reason we never took sandwiches, probably because with meat, butter, cheese etc. all rationed there was nothing to put inside them! At about this time, however, on the pretext that pilots were getting over-tired and were having accidents by carrying on for a full day without eating, the ATA Medical Officer, Dr Buchanan Barbour, managed to persuade the Ministry to allocate ATA a supply of 2 oz bars of Cadbury's Dairy Milk chocolate which in wartime, was luxury indeed! In order to qualify for what was then a twopenny bar, one had to present one's ferry chit for the day in question to the Pool Adjutant, who then duly

unlocked a cupboard in his office and issued one. Occasionally one got lunch anyway or simply forgot to eat the chocolate and then, in my case anyway, it got stowed away in the metal locker where we kept our flying gear and where, unbelievably, mice sometimes managed to get in and eat it, silver paper and all!

Whenever possible Ferry Control, when allocating jobs to the various Ferry Pools, would issue return trips to match outward ones so as to enable pilots to get back to their base without involving long trips in taxi aircraft. Obviously the more types of aircraft a pilot was cleared to fly, the better the chance of getting a round trip. An example of such a day from my log book reads: Taxi aircraft White Waltham to Brooklands, Wellington HX598 Brooklands to Little Rissington, Spitfire EP410 Little Rissington to Llandow, Mosquito DD671 St. Athan to Ford, Mustang AG505 Ford to Lichfield, Taxi Puss Moth Lichfield to Castle Bromwich, Wellington X9707 Castle Bromwich to White Waltham.

On this day I took off from Brooklands in the first Wellington at 10.45 and arrived back at White Waltham at 18.05, having spent four hours and five minutes in the air. Considering the essential formalities

No.1 Ferry Pool Ferry pilots and Instructors. L-R; 'Bill' Harben, W J White, Jim Mollison, P L Burnett, Joan Hughes, Stewart Keith-Jopp, 'Ben' Warne, 'Doc' Whitehurst, J Shoesmith, 'Red' Imes, R H Henderson, Harry Ellis, ELC, Klemens Dlugaszewski, Vic Pieper.

involved at each stopping place, the fact that aircraft were rarely signed up until the pilot actually appeared, that aircraft dispersal areas were often far removed from the Maintenance Unit reception hut and that this was a Saturday, this must be considered an exceptional day. Especially so in this case as it was necessary to persuade someone to produce transport for the four-mile drive from Llandow airfield to St. Athan. In spite of this the longest time I spent on the ground was 1 hr 15 mins at Ford, where I had not been expected, and where as a result a daily inspection had not been carried out. The shortest time was at Castle Bromwich where, warned of my arrival, they were waiting to get rid of the repaired aircraft and go home. Here only ten minutes elapsed between landing in the Puss Moth and taking off again in the Wellington.

Days like this were only possible in fine weather during the summer and, if this was something in the nature of an initiative test, it was to me a thoroughly enjoyable one. There was enormous satisfaction to be gained by thinking back at the end of the day, over obstacles overcome and the aircraft one had managed to move.

axi aircraft at *'hite Waltham.* *nson and* *airchilds.*

Another notably long day that summer was one in which, after moving two Spitfires and a Hornet Moth interspersed with three Fairchild taxi trips, I got back to White Waltham around half past four.

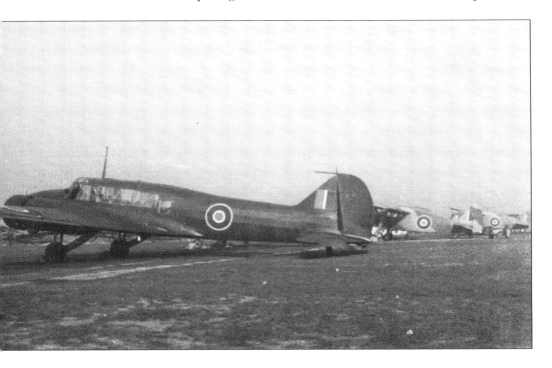

I had just gone to the Mess for a cup of tea and was in the process of contemplating how to pass the evening when over the Tannoy came the message: "Pilots Curtis and Newmark to Operations please." Some priority Spitfires had just come on the books. And so, instead of an early evening, it was out again in a Fairchild, this time to Benson where we collected our aircraft for Sealand. Once there we were met by an Anson from Hawarden which, when the rest of the party arrived, took Herbie Newmark and I to Shawbury where there was a Whitley waiting to be delivered to Abingdon. Herbie had the chit for this while I was to be his passenger. By the time we left Shawbury it was ten past eight. When pilots were out for a long day like this the operations staff at base always did their level best to see that they were collected. This evening they had persuaded 'Molotov' Watson from the headquarters staff to come out in

Bill White, 'Whitey' Senior Operations Officer for No.1 Ferry Pool at White Waltham.

a Fairchild to collect us. We were indeed glad to see him and eventually got back to White Waltham around 10 pm. For me this day had continued virtually non-stop for twelve hours.

These are just examples from my own experience, but many log books would have had similar tales to tell. When one was sent out like this relatively late in the day, one's first reaction was to blame the operations staff for picking on you for the dirty jobs. The answer was of course that they didn't, although there was an understandable tendency to pick willing pilots who would make least excuses. Sometimes, when we returned in the afternoon, we would find 'Whitey,' No. 1 F.P's senior Operations Officer, hanging out of the window of the operations room as we lugged our parachutes back to the parachute store.

"You've had it!" he would shout. "Priority Spits for Sealand" or Prestwick or wherever else it might be, but then more kindly: "I'm awfully sorry, but there is no one else."

"What about old so-and-so?" you would ask hopefully, catching sight of another pilot in the distance. But there was always some reason why 'old so-and-so' couldn't go and, in the end, there was nothing for it but to go to the Mess for a snack, then to your locker for a fresh set of maps and to the Met. Office for the latest forecast. The Met. forecast was largely a formality as with priority aircraft you had to take off and go as far as you could, even if there was little chance of reaching your destination. The operations staff undertook the chore of ringing up one's wife or digs to say that you would be late for supper or would not be back at all that night.

A page from the No.1 Ferry Pilot's Pool Operations Book.

CHAPTER 16

HALIFAX TRAINING

By 1942 the number of four-engined aircraft required to be delivered by ATA had increased and more ATA pilots were needed to move them; the ATA Advanced Flying Training School was therefore extended to include four-engine training. As one might have expected, RAF bombers were in short supply so the aircraft allotted to ATA for training was a Halifax, more of which were being built at that time than any other British bomber.

Pilots were recommended for Class 5 (four-engined conversion) by Ferry Pool Commanders. Situated as I was in an all male Ferry Pool, I was lucky to have had in Frankie Francis a commanding officer who was prepared to put forward for the first time a woman. It was lucky too that A.R.O. Macmillan was still our Chief Instructor as he too was unbiased in his approach to women pilots; I have a strong feeling that the CFI who succeeded him at the end of the year would not have let my name go through. As far as I was concerned, therefore, I was grateful to be in the right place at the right time and with the right C.O.; there were C.O's who would not even have women in their Ferry Pools.

The main doubt, I was told afterwards, was whether women would have sufficient physical strength to cope. Even so, like many other

Handley Page Halifax

firsts in ATA, nothing about it came easily. The first ATA training aircraft had been a Focke-Wulf Condor, brought over from Denmark by its peacetime pilot Captain Hanson when the Germans invaded. However it was never used as such, partly because of maintenance difficulties and

also because shortly after its arrival at White Waltham it overshot on wet grass and was written off. After this training reverted to doing two or three landings from the second pilot's seat in a ferry aircraft along with another ATA pilot. It was not until 1942 that ATA acquired its own four-engined aircraft for training. This aircraft, BD191, was one of the first Mk. II Halifaxes built by the London Aircraft Production Group at Leavesden, where it was housed whilst being used by ATA. The ATA instructor given responsibility for training was a very well-liked Pole, Klemens Dlugaszewski. 'Dluga,' as we called him, had been flying for twenty years before escaping from Poland to fly with ATA. He had been one of Poland's first commercial pilots, joining the airline LOT at its foundation in 1929. All this put him way ahead of us not only in flying, but

lemens lugaszewski, under member the Polish irline LOT.

in experience of life. In ATA he was respected for his modesty, gentleness and his quiet sense of humour. In the years ahead I grew immensely fond of him and came to rely on his kindness, stability and common sense in what had become a disturbed and unstable world.

He was also remembered for the example he set by his strong sense of personal discipline. Leavesden at the time consisted of one 1,000-yard runway, one end of which sloped down towards the hangars where the Halifax was kept. It was not a suitable place for pilots to practise circuits and landings. Whenever the aircraft was serviceable the two of us on the course at the time would go over to Leavesden with Dluga, who would then fly the aircraft to some RAF airfield with a runway roughly into wind where they were willing to take us. We went to Bovingdon, Bassingbourn and on one occasion to Hampsted Norreys in the hills west of Reading. I particularly remember this occasion because, after a couple of circuits, Dluga said I was ready for solo but wouldn't let me go because he said he considered the runway was too short; the spotlight was on him as much as on me. To me this was a very harassing period for, not only was I faced with possible failure, which I would have minded about inordinately, but at the back of my mind was the knowledge that any mistakes or failures, even if not of my own making, could result in an official decision that four-engined aircraft were not for women.

I was posted to the school for Class 5 conversion on September 24th 1942. The 23rd, my last day of ferrying for No. 1 Ferry Pool, had consisted of a Hurricane from Langley to 20 MU at Aston Down and another from Aston Down to Hunsden where a Fairchild waited to collect me. After a cup of tea I was leaving the Mess when I met Bruce Campbell, and there in the sunlight on the steps of the Mess he told me that a mutual friend, Armstrong Payn, who had also been at Hamble, had died whilst on sick leave from No. 2 Ferry Pool at Bristol. Bruce was about to take a Fairchild to Mount Farm to collect someone who had delivered an aircraft there so, not wanting to be alone, I went with him for the ride, sealing a friendship with another highly individual character, that lasted until his death many years later. Armstrong's funeral, which I very much wanted to attend, was scheduled for the 26th but, for the first time since I had joined the school, the Halifax was serviceable and the weather good. On the advice of my C.O. but sick at heart I therefore went with Bill Simms, the other pupil, to Leavesden with Dluga. From there we flew to Bassingbourn where Simms, who had already started the course, did most of the flying and I only took the controls briefly as we returned to Leavesden in deteriorating weather.

It was a foggy autumn. Between bad weather and unserviceability, flying was spasmodic to say the least of it, and it was a week before I next flew in the Halifax. This time we went to Bovingdon, where I made four dual circuits. The aircraft was certainly a lump to handle but not, I felt, all that heavier than a Wellington; neither could it be allowed to get out of trim. It was the ailerons, I found, that called for anything

5/10/42.
rs Roosevelt on
r official visit
atting to
merican women
lots.
ight:
uline Gower,
rs Roosevelt,
erald
Erlanger.
eft: Mrs O. P.
. Anderson
JSA),
nknown,
aomi Allen,
nn Wood
JSA)

approaching brute strength. I did the odd dual circuit on two more occasions, the last on October 11th after which, because of bad weather and more unserviceability, there was no more flying until the 27th. I filled the intermediate time by ferrying the odd Spitfire or Wellington for No. 1 Ferry Pool. On the day before the course resumed Mrs Roosevelt came to White Waltham on what the Press called a 'hustle tour.' Accompanied by Mrs Churchill, she was here to study the activities of women in wartime Britain. It was a pouring wet day and Mrs Roosevelt, an umbrella held over her head, was conducted by Commodore d'Erlanger and Pauline Gower down a line of newly-joined American pilots who had been brought to White Waltham to meet her. I had been asked to stand under the wing of a Halifax brought in for the occasion, which kept some of the rain off, and when they came past I was inevitably introduced as the first woman to be trained on four-engined bombers.

Next day the papers latched on to this and, regardless of the fact that I had not as yet even gone solo, published headlines such as: 'Mrs. Roosevelt meets Halifax Girl Pilot' and 'Girl Flies Halifax' – the sort of build-up that can destroy. This added to my already heavy mental load as I felt I wasn't doing particularly well on the course. Next day,

ELC in the spacious cockpit of a Halifax.

however, the weather had improved and the Halifax was serviceable and so, after an interval of two weeks, the aircraft was once again taken to Bovingdon where Dluga got out leaving me and flight engineer F.E.H. Lees to get on with it. I remember that as we taxied in, Dluga and Sims stood at the end of the runway saluting! It was not for me so much a moment of achievement as one of acute relief that at last, the first bridge had been crossed.

That night at White Waltham the instructors were holding a party. With this flight under my belt I could for a brief period at least relax and enjoy the sweetness of this small success. Life for the moment was very good. Four days later I completed six more solo landings. This time Jim Bain, ATA's senior flight engineer, flew with me so that he could counter any possible objections from other flight engineers to flying with a woman. But this was by no means the end of the story. Seven solo landings would normally have been ample to clear a pilot for ferrying but in my case, ATA's new Chief Flying Instructor had made an arbitrary decision that in my case ten solo landings must be made before I could be cleared. But the Halifax now went unserviceable yet again. Simms was declared 'cleared' and went back to his Ferry Pool to ferry Halifaxes but I, with seven solo landings, returned to my Ferry Pool cleared as before only for singles and twins. After every peak comes a trough – success in this case had been very fleeting. I was told nothing. Had politics intervened? ATA's new CFI was clearly not on my side. But back at No. 1 Ferry Pool, with the problem of coping with short winter days and November fogs, all was soon forgotten as four-engine training came to a stop until February 1943, when it restarted on a more organised basis at RAF Pocklington. Here a joint training flight under the command of a Squadron Leader had been formed to give conversion courses to pilots and flight engineers of both 41 Group Maintenance Command, who provided the test crews at maintenance units, and ATA. Flight Captain R.H. Henderson, a senior ATA pilot, joined the flight on behalf of ATA. The day after he arrived, however, the Squadron Leader was posted, leaving Henderson in the unusual position for a civilian of being in charge of an RAF Flight of some thirty airmen and NCOs from 41 Group. I arrived at Pocklington on 11th February and, once again due to weather, we had a slow start. Pocklington was an operational station so, as was usual, women were not allowed in the main Mess. I was therefore given a room in the WAAF Officers' house which was some way off, leaving me with no contact with male aircrew on the same course except when flying. Flying, when it started, went reasonably well and I went solo again on my second flight. Unusually for us, at Pocklington the Halifax was armed and carried an air gunner even for practice circuits,

LC takes off in Halifax.

and when it was someone else's turn to fly I would wander down the fuselage and sit in any unoccupied seat intended for an air gunner. 'Hendy' was a great one for crosswind landings and we had some hectic moments when he demonstrated two and three-engine approaches.

The radio equipment fitted consisted of old TR9HF/RT, the quality of which was so poor that half the time it was more trouble than it was worth to use it. Nevertheless it had to be used to call for taxi, take-off and landing clearance etc. As ferry aircraft never carried radio, this too was something new.

I finished the course on 25th February, finally cleared for ferrying Halifaxes, but all was not yet plain sailing. I was all too conscious that a woman flying a Halifax was 'news' and that if a good story could be made out of any small incident over the bar in the evening, no opportunity would be lost for embroidering it. My first ferry trip was in Halifax DG303, specially dropped at Mount Farm for delivery to 295 Squadron TAF at the large but undulating grass airfield of Netheravon. The aircraft had been brought from Prestwick by Rear Admiral Boucher who was ATA's Commanding Officer of Northern Area. A pioneer of the Fleet Air Arm, he had retired from the Royal Navy in 1939 and, when he joined ATA, started off in the EFTS like any other newcomer and worked his way through the school. The ferry trip passed without incident and back at White Waltham I immediately volunteered to take a taxi Anson to collect pilots from Middle Wallop, Ibsley and Thorney Island. After the Halifax the Anson felt like a Moth! By the time ATA closed in November 1945 I had ferried 222 Halifaxes, 109 Stirlings, lesser numbers of Lancasters, Liberators and one Fortress.

In the middle of April 1943, the airfield at White Waltham was declared 'unserviceable'. Someone in the Ministry of Aircraft Production had decided that the grass needed reseeding and with the seed, a top dressing of fertiliser was applied. All went well until some dry weather arrived and the ground hardened, aircraft started getting punctures. School aircraft which were making circuits and landings were the first to be hit and as a result flying school activities had to be stopped. Investigation revealed that old iron had been mixed with the fertiliser which included such things as knives, forks, tin-openers and even pieces of broken glass. As long as the ground was soft these had remained

D U P L I C A T E.

AIR TRANSPORT AUXILIARY

FLIGHT AUTHORIZATION CARD No. W.5.

First Officer (Rank) E.L. CURTIS Miss (Name) is hereby empowered to authorize his own cross-country flights in accordance with A.M.O.'s 394 and 459.

Class	Date	Signature		Class	Date	Signature
1.	14.11.40	P.M.		5 Hal:	25.2.43	P.M.
2.	14.11.40	P.M.		5 STIR.	1.8.43	lw
3.	14.11.40	P.M.		5 FoRT.	20.9.43	lw
4.	15.10.41	P.M.		3+	1941.	lw
4+.	12.4.42	P.M.		2+	1942	lw
R.T.	25.2.43	P.M.		V.H.F.	25.2.45.	O.C. A.F.T.S.

AUXILIARY

Chief Instructor.

My Flight Authorisation Card detailing the classes of aircraft I was permitted to fly including the four-engined bombers.

buried, but when it dried out the extraneous bodies became set as if in concrete, resistant to tyres coming in contact with than and as a result, the airfield was closed.

With the closure of the airfield, No.1 Ferry Pool, in order to enable them to continue ferrying, removed their Anson and Fairchild taxi aircraft to a nearby forced-landing field at Waltham St Lawrence which was called Forty Acres. Here although take-off loads had to be reduced, the Pool could at least continue to operate. To deal with the situation unemployed school students, ground staff, ferry pilots and even some of the top brass were given buckets and cardboard boxes. Forming a line stretching across the whole airfield they scoured every inch of ground, picking up anything that came to light. This did not prove to be enough and eventually some giant magnets were obtained and drawn over the field behind a tractor. To start with a marked off area of ground was cleared so that after a gap of some ten days it became possible to resume at least a limited amount of flying. Kidlington, another grass airfield, had been issued with the same fertiliser but were lucky enough to discover the content before it was spread.

For the ferry pool, buses and trucks were laid on to transport pilots, engineers, parachutes and aircraft servicing crews to and from Forty Acres where the combination of short take-off, rough grass and warm weather restricted loads carried by both Fairchilds and Ansons. For ferry pilots this meant that after a day out ferrying, there was often a long wait before transport was available to take than back to White Waltham. For some this provided an opportunity to call in at the Plough, a nearby pub renowned for its hospitality which has now sadly been turned into a private house.

My log book shows no take-offs or landings from White Waltham between 15th April and the 2nd May. During this period I see that on 20th of April I delivered one of the taxi Ansons in to Forty Acres, and made several Fairchild flights in and out.

In August 1943 I flew my first Stirling and between then and 1945, flew some 109 of them. This was an aircraft well liked by ATA pilots who flew them with everything in their favour - at light weight, low altitude and more often than not, in mint condition. The Stirling was the only one of the three British four-engined bombers to be designed from scratch for four engines. It went into use in August 1940 and although unsuccessful as a bomber, it remained in service throughout the war. It had been designed round a 112ft Sunderland wing but the Air Ministry insisted, as on other bombers, that its wingspan must not be more than l00 feet 'to conform' they said 'with existing hangar dimensions'. This meant that both wings and flaps had to be redesigned to meet the specified take-off and landing distances which were no longer being met. A half-scale wooden model was therefore built to access handling characteristics, which was still on view in the hangar at Rochester in 1943, but was later written off in a crash at Stradishall. Tests on the mock-up showed that take-off and landing distances were still too long. To remedy this, wing incidence was increased by 3 degrees by lengthening the undercarriage legs, thereby increasing the ground angle of the whole aircraft. No.1 Ferry Pool at White Waltham was responsible for clearing Stirlings from Short's factory at Rochester and it was on an

Short Stirling

aircraft I took from there that the following incident occurred. On a day of early morning mist rising slowly to low stratus, my job for the day was to take a Stirling from Rochester to Hawarden. After waiting for the weather to improve, I left with my flight engineer from White Waltham for Rochester in a Fairchild with the cloud still at around 800 feet. Rochester airfield was in the centre of the London balloon barrage and could only be approached through a lane that was left permanently open because most of the balloons were fixtures. The position of the balloons therefore rarely changed nevertheless, we were instructed before going to Rochester to check the position of the lane. I however, having been through it a number of times recently, on this occasion thought I knew it well enough and didn't need to check.

I therefore flew the Fairchild in and the Stirling out through the lane I thought I knew. It was only on returning to White Waltham that I was told that the pilot returning the Fairchild to White Waltham, thinking he was following the lane I had used, found himself face to face with a balloon cable whereupon he circled it and landed in a field. It was only after he landed that the low cloud dissolved and the London balloons appeared in all their glory. The balloon lane, I now learnt, had been changed the previous day so the Stirling as well as the Fairchild I flew must have flown through the barrage, somehow missing the cables! For me the thought that I had flown through the barrage both in the Fairchild and in the Stirling was punishment enough!

In the latter part of the war Stirlings played a major role towing gliders and No.1 Ferry Pool took a number in and out of No.34 Satellite field at Woburn, where yokes and release gear were fitted to enable them to tow gliders.

A Stirling glider tug.

CHAPTER 17

FIDO AND THE HALIFAX

In February 1944 I had the doubtful honour of making what was ,in all probability, the only ATA landing on *FIDO*. This was the code used for 'Fog Investigation and Dispersal Operation' , a system designed to clear a hole in fog or low cloud over a runway to allow aircraft returning from operations to land at their home base. Burners for this were laid on either side of some 1,000 yards of runway, from which pressurised petrol was burnt in blowlamp fashion to generate enormous quantities of heat, sufficient to disperse cloud or fog up to some 400 feet.

In February 1943 Graveley, a Pathfinder station near Huntingdon, was one of the first stations to be brought into use experimentally. The first emergency landings by aircraft returning from operations had taken place in November that year and it was to Graveley that in February 1944, on a clear winter's day of blue sky and ground haze, that I was given the job of taking a new Halifax from Radlett. The visibility at Radlett was reasonable, but when I rang Gravely before I left for a weather 'actual,' we were told that visibility due to ground haze was such that they couldn't accept us. ATA pilots, however, were empowered to authorise their own flights and, provided the airfield wasn't actually unserviceable, could make their own decision as to weather. Since it was only a question of ground haze and I could return to Radlett without risk if I found I was unable to land at Gravely, I decided to take off and see for myself what it was like there. From overhead Graveley the runways showed up through the haze and I could see the landing "T" which, in spite of negligible wind, marked the short runway. Nevertheless I set off on a circuit from which landing must inevitably end with letting down into the haze. On final approach the runway became visible but the indications were that I was not adequately lined up for the early touchdown necessary in view of its limited length. I therefore opened up the engines and went round for another try.

Unbeknown to me the airfield controllers were waiting for an excuse for a practice light-up of their fog dispersal system, so when I

A Lancaster lands within the fires of the FIDO equipped runway at Graveley.

appeared they immediately changed the 'T' on to the long runway and lit the first few hundred yards of burners. I would have happily settled for the long runway without FIDO, especially as the smoke from the initial light-up made the haze several degrees worse. In the event I made my approach through a dense black cloud, guided by the parallel bars of light from the burning petrol, touching down before sufficient heat had built up to disperse the haze. After landing the 'follow me' van took me to a far dispersal where unusually, it waited to take me back to the Control Tower. Having been told previously not to come to Graveley I was feeling distinctly sheepish as I climbed the steps to the control room, but here I was and they had at enormous expense, lit up their FIDO to get me in. I was expecting to get a serious telling off. Instead, I was asked with genuine interest how I had found the landing and I was able to answer truthfully that, in spite of the smoke, it had been entirely straightforward because of the parallel bars of light. In retrospect the most frightening thing about it was the thought that if for any reason the aircraft swung off the runway, it could not have failed to cross the line of intense and living flame. The Halifax had been sufficiently heavy to ride the turbulence but not so the Fairchild that arrived a few minutes later to pick me and my flight engineer up. The heat and rising air meant that it was only with great difficulty that it had managed to get down on the runway at all.

On 30th July 1944, I was amongst a group of pilots on the terrace outside the Mess at White Waltham waiting for the clouds to clear, when we heard bombers overhead. This was not an unusual occurrence as in that stage in the war after the D-Day landings, formations of bombers often passed over at low level en route to daylight bombing raids on the other side of the Channel. On this occasion however the bombers were flying unusually low and because of low cloud we couldn't see them, but then one broke cloud flying at circuit height. As we watched, it lowered its undercarriage before disappearing to the south. When it reappeared it was lined up as if for landing on the south-east to north-west run, the shortest on the airfield which pointed directly towards the Great Western Railway. Surely, we said to one another, it's not going to attempt a landing! But in the event this was exactly what it was about to do. Everyone in the Mess now came out on to the terrace and in the building, faces were glued to windows. Meanwhile those of us already outside simply held our breath and watched as the aircraft touched down a good half way across the airfield, leaving no possible doubt as to what the end was going to be. We could only assume that the pilot had not appreciated that there was a railway cutting between the airfield and the flat field on the other side of the railway.

History, however, tells a different story. The aircraft was from No.420 Squadron, a Canadian Halifax Squadron based at Tolthorpe in Yorkshire, and was returning from a low level bombing raid on Bayeaux. With engine problems as well as bad weather the pilot was looking for somewhere to land. Through broken cloud the pilot had seen White Waltham and it was here that he had decided to land. By the time he had lined up however, he had realised that he had chosen the wrong approach, but with insufficient power to overshoot, he had no option but to continue with the landing.

To those watching, the aircraft seemed to reach the railway cutting at considerable speed with its undercarriage still down where it disappeared from view. The fire and crash crews who had seen the accident coming were out almost before the bomber came to rest. A few pilots and flight engineers rushed to their cars and drove out to see if there was anything they could do to help. Flames had already broken out on the starboard wing, but by spraying foam the fire crew was able to keep the flames under control. Some set about entering the aircraft to extricate the crew but with injuries and flying equipment to remove this was not an easy task. It was whilst the helpers were working inside the aircraft that a bystander drew their attention to a bomb that had rolled out onto the railway track. It was then that the 'helpers', unaware that the aircraft was returning from a raid, realised for the first time that the aircraft could have been 'bombed up'.

Meanwhile a train was approaching the crash from the direction of Maidenhead. This was a long, straight piece of track and fortunately the driver had been able to see from way back that the line was blocked and had pulled up - but only just in time. One of the helpers therefore rushed out, shouting to the train driver to reverse, which with some reluctance he did.

Of the seven crew carried in the Halifax, all but two of were uninjured and survived the crash. The most seriously injured was the RAF wireless operator who also survived the crash, but died shortly afterwards. It was only with considerable difficulty that with the star-board wing blazing, the rear gunner, who was unconscious and badly injured was got out. As the most difficult member of the crew to extri-cate he was the last to be freed. With all the crew rescued and as there was little more the helpers could do, both the fire and crash crews with-drew leaving the fire to take its course. Shortly afterwards a column of smoke rose into the sky and minutes later, there was an explosion in which the aircraft disintegrated.

Meanwhile, news of the bomb had reached the operations room from whence pilots standing around were sent out to move aircraft parked on the tarmac to the east side of the airfield, further away from any exploding bombs. I was given the task of taxiing an Anson to the other side of the field and it was just after I had parked it, that an explo-sion took place. This was followed by a jagged piece of metal about four inches square landing at my feet, that for a long time I kept as a souvenir. The railway embankment had deflected the blast upward and the only damage to the main building, which was relatively close to the blast, was a broken window. According to the Maidenhead Advertiser, damage to the railway tracks delayed trains to Reading and the West but within two hours, an up and down service was restored and by 2.30 pm, trains were again running to timetable. "Great presence of mind was shown by the driver of the troop train" the Maidenhead Advertiser wrote, "which was approaching the spot where the 'plane crashed. He managed to avert what might have proved a further disaster by pulling up within a few yards of the burning 'plane and backing the train out of danger." Awards to ATA men for bravery included two MBEs, a George Medal and two British Empire Medals, one of which went to the Station Fire Officer. There were also three recommendations for gallantry.

CHAPTER 18

TYPHOON ACCIDENT

We had been flying Typhoons since 1942 but early ones with the Sabre I and II engines were not popular with ATA pilots. In the development stage there had been a number of accidents both in the RAF and also with test pilots. A high frequency vibration, particularly marked in aircraft with three-bladed propellers, was rumoured to have devastating effects on male pilots which did nothing to relieve our fears. There were problems too with the 24-cylinder H-type sleeve-valve Napier Sabre engines, which made life difficult even for ferry pilots. Starting the Mark I and II's engine with cartridge starters could be the first problem – even the ATA Notes included complicated starting instructions detailing the number of priming shots that should be given with differing oil temperatures. It was essential to arrive at exactly the right degree of doping because if over-doped, plugs had to be removed and the cylinder primed with oil before further attempts to start were made. Starting was particularly difficult in winter when the oil was cold. All pilots who flew Typhoons must have memories of firing off cartridge after cartridge at some time or other in fruitless attempts to get the engine going, to the desperation of both pilot and ground crew.

Stopping the engine could also produce further problems. Initially we were instructed to idle the engine for a full two minutes before cutting the fuel. Later we were told that it must be idled for only a few seconds. The early instructions to ground staff said that the engine must be run daily and "if it is known that the engine is not going to be run within 48 hours it must be inhibited." To those of us with little mechanical knowledge, all these instructions seemed highly complicated and not a little frustrating; how much more so for the unfortunate ground crews at Maintenance Units. It was later in the war that in a Typhoon, I had my only major accident. On 22 April 1944 I had returned from two days leave to a full day's ferrying – an old Wellington from White Waltham to Brooklands, a Warwick from Brooklands to the de Havilland propeller division at Hatfield and a Mosquito from

Ann Blackwell in Typhoon.

Hatfield to 10 MU Hullavington where a Fairchild was waiting to take me for my last trip to Aston Down to collect a Typhoon. The aircraft, JP686, was one of an early batch which had been called in by the parent factory at Langley for modification. I had been told to ring White Waltham after I had delivered it for transport back to base.

It was late in the afternoon when I approached Langley and being a clear day, the close-hauled balloons marking the balloon lane were clearly visible. The open lane was approximately west to east and more or less dead across a light wind. I was approaching from the west and about to make a straight-in approach when, glancing at the wind-sock, I decided that this would be slightly downwind; I therefore changed my plans, continuing in a wide circuit outside the balloons to the other end of the lane. If I had landed as originally planned,

curtailing my flying time by a couple of minutes, I might well have landed safely. As it was, I was about to turn in to the north-east end of the balloon lane when the engine quietly faded. A quick check of the instrument panel showed that the red fuel pressure light was on, signifying a fuel failure.

I knew there was plenty of fuel on board so automatically went through the motions of changing tanks, but to no avail. I was still at a reasonable height and, but for the balloons, could have turned directly into the airfield and landed safely. But the high rate of descent resulting from the undercarriage and flaps which were set for landing prevented me reaching the balloon lane. There was a sizable field just outside the airfield alongside the railway which, apart from some trees at the edge of it, appeared to be a reasonable place to make a forced landing. I therefore set about raising the undercarriage using the hand pump. When it was nearly up I paused, waiting to see how we were placed as regards the trees.

Now for the first time there was time to consider what was happening. I again looked round the cockpit for some clue to the engine failure – something, anything I had left undone – but nothing came to

A female ATA pilot lands a Typhoon.

mind. Being an early Typhoon, it did not have the usual sliding roof, entry to the cockpit being by a car-type door with a wind-down window. I wound down the window, more from a feeling of claustrophobia than anything else, and tightened my harness. After clearing the trees my attention focussed on the problem of landing and nearing the ground, I held off for what must have been a few seconds, waiting for the aircraft to stall; I then recalled that the field ended in gravel pits which were now out of sight behind the engine cowling, so changed my mind and 'flew' onto the ground. I must have touched down at something like 100 mph and immediately the huge ventral cooling scoop so characteristic of the Typhoon, bit into the earth. The aircraft flicked tail over nose on to its back. I learnt afterwards that the aircraft had turned over with such force that the tail had broken off and flown forward a further twenty or so yards. The next thing I was aware of was hanging upside down on my straps, protected from the ground by the Perspex cabin roof and with a slow ticking coming from the hot engine.

As the forced landing had resulted from fuel failure the risk of fire must have been minimal, but my immediate reaction was to get clear of the aircraft. I undid my straps and tried to get out of the window in the door, but couldn't make it; then I remembered my parachute and when I had released this I found I could just squeeze through. As I emerged people started to arrive, as they will out of nowhere, and amongst them was a doctor. I had gashes on the left side of my face and on my left leg. I had indeed been lucky for the aircraft had had a large Mark III gunsight protruding into the cockpit at eye level which in flight had been inches from my head and which if I had I hit it straight on, could have caused permanent disfigurement. In retrospect I think that the starboard leg of the undercarriage was probably trailing and catching the ground first, probably jerked the aircraft to the right. As I had been thrown to the left I was saved from serious injury. The doctor put a temporary bandage on my head and told me that it would have to be stitched.

In due course the airfield ambulance arrived, the crew muttering that because it was Saturday afternoon they had been unable to leave the airfield. Once I was on board they announced that they were taking me to Slough Emergency Hospital. I however, had other ideas;

the Royal Canadian Hospital at Taplow was ATA's 'home' hospital and I was determined to go there. The ambulance driver, still muttering about it being Saturday afternoon, said that although it was only some five miles away he couldn't go that far, so he took me back to the airfield where I still refused to relax until things went my way. After sundry conferences they eventually gave in and off we set for Taplow. By the time we reached Cliveden they were fed up with me and left me to get out on my own, so after thanking them for bringing me I walked up on my own to the reception counter. Would they be kind enough, I asked, to sew up my head?

By now I should have known that the answer would be: "It's Saturday afternoon and we don't know if there is a doctor available." There was a row of chairs, probably intended for visitors, in the waiting area where I was told to sit and wait. Here a lady who was making a Saturday afternoon visit to the hospital with a friend took me under her wing.

"You young things!" she said; "whatever will you get up to next?" I explained that I had been in an aircraft accident and that I had been told that my head needed stitching, whereupon she introduced me to her friend, who was sitting next to me, while she went off to look for a doctor. We talked of this and that and I remember pulling up my trouser leg to show her an impressive gash on my left leg. With mud from the field on my clothes together with blood from my head, I must have been quite an impressive sight but no one appeared to notice anything unusual. Eventually Lady Astor, for that was who the lady turned out to be, returned with a doctor and I asked him if I could go home when they had dressed my head; when told "No," I insisted in them ringing up my digs to say that I would not be back.

The room I was allocated was off a corridor connecting two large wards in the surgical wing of the hospital. The ward nearest me contained casualties from the campaign in Italy, many of whom were convalescent and up and about to the extent that their plasters and crutches would allow. One of them would bring round to those still in bed the last meal of the day, and so it was that at around half past six, one of them burst into my room asking how I was and why I was there? He was somewhat offended to find me not very forthcoming.

The truth of the matter was that this was about the best opportunity I had had for rest since the war began! After four years of almost non-stop flying, tiredness had at last taken over. At last I hadn't a worry in the world, I need stir myself for nothing and my relaxation was complete, so I just slept and slept. Sleep was in fact my principal occupation for the following week, to the unsettlement of the nurse who seemed to think there was something almost indecent about turning off the light as early as 9 o'clock. Being on home ground I did not lack for visitors, letters or even flowers. As I felt little worse for my mishap, I could thoroughly enjoy the fuss. The radio in the next-door ward was on most of the time and if I felt like company, I had only to leave the door of the room open and occupants of the ward next door would wander in and out. Apparently the same sort of thing happened in the medical wing, but there it was not appreciated as most of the patients were not feeling too good!

At the end of the ward next door there was a veranda on to which beds were pushed on sunny days, so by Wednesday I was being pushed out there with the others. The first day I recall someone saying in a surprised tone of voice: "You did look ill the day you came in" as if that was the last way one should look when admitted to hospital. But I found the Canadian Hospital a remarkable and happy place. Sometimes of an evening, those capable of propelling themselves that far would go down to the Feathers, a public house a little way down the road. I looked forward very much to the time when I was up and able to join them but unfortunately this never happened. On Thursday the doctor came round and told me that I was to be discharged the following day. As I hadn't as yet even got up I felt this was definitely one below the belt! Apart from visiting the Feathers I wanted to see something of the grounds of this well-known country house. If I was well enough to leave hospital next day I decided, I was well enough to get up now. So up I got, dressed, borrowed a bicycle which was leaning against the wall outside, and went off on a tour of the wooded grounds which sloped down to the Thames where I remember seeing some very colourful pheasants. Having made my tour I returned, put the bicycle back where I had found it, undressed, got back into bed and had my supper brought as usual by someone from the next-door ward.

What in fact had happened was that the entire staff of the 7th Canadian Hospital, under whose care I had been, were being sent overseas and they didn't want to leave any unnecessary bodies around for the 11th Canadian Hospital who were taking their place. That night whilst I was sleeping off my bicycle ride, quite a party was, I heard later on, held in which all the medicinal brandy was drunk. I was sad indeed to have missed it! Next day I got up and dressed and a car was sent from White Waltham to collect me. At the airfield I picked up my car and, after calling at my digs, went off to spend a week with Margie Fairweather and her babe at Kidmore End. This had been arranged to provide both convalescence for me and company for Margie, whose husband Douglas had been killed three weeks earlier.

He had volunteered to collect an ambulance case from Prestwick which required urgent treatment at the Canadian Hospital; the weather however was appalling. In low cloud and rain somewhere over the Irish Sea the Anson came down and both Douglas and the nurse were lost. After many escapes in similar weather his luck had at last run out. Margie in due course returned to flying but was herself killed four months later, when making a forced landing in a Proctor after an engine failure. Thus passed one of the ablest of ATA's first eight women pilots.

CHAPTER 19

FOR THE INVASION

At the time of the invasion in 1944 two Group Support Units (GSUs) were set up in order to keep the Second Tactical Air Force supplied with the aircraft they needed; these were No. 83 at Redhill and No. 84 at Aston Down. No. 1 Ferry Pool supplied aircraft to 83 GSU where they were held until collected by the RAF. On 13th June, exactly a week after D-Day, the first German V1 flying bombs were launched over England. One fell at Bethnal Green, causing the first deaths and casualties, but the main attack opened a few days later when the Guards Chapel in Wellington Barracks received a direct hit during the Sunday morning service and was completely destroyed.

The entirely random nature of the new bombing and the fact that there was no foreseeable end to any particular raid imposed new tensions. In the inimitable words of Winston Churchill, "dawn brought no relief and cloud no comfort." The man going home in the evening never knew what he would find; whilst his wife, alone all day with the children, could not be certain of his safe return. The impersonal nature of the missile made individuals on the ground helpless. There was little anyone could do, no enemy that could be seen to be shot down.

Mustangs of a Polish squadron, part of the force assembled to combat the V-1 flying bomb threat.

On 20th June an Inter-Service Committee was set up to plan measures to be taken against 'V' weapons – for the 'V2' rocket was already anticipated. The original plan was for fighters to aim at intercepting the bombs either over the Channel or in the belt between the coast and the London balloons. No. 11 Group Fighter Command provided eight day fighter and four night fighter squadrons equipped with Typhoons, Tempests, Spitfires, Mosquitos and Polish Mustangs for chasing the V1s; however most of the bombs destroyed fell over land. In spite of attempts to wipe out launching sites of the flying bombs, the menace of V1s did not end until the sites were captured by the Allied invasion force. Redhill now came under what had become the direct route for the V1s – or 'Doodlebugs', as they were now called – a track that had come to be known as 'Bomb Alley.' It was therefore decided that the GSU must be moved, the new site selected being a grass field near Bognor.

The first time I became aware of this was on 24th June; after taking a Halifax to Linton-on-Ouse in Yorkshire and a Whitley from Honeybourne to Llandow, my final task was to get transport to St. Athan where a Mustang was waiting to be taken to Redhill. At Redhill, before I had even stopped the engine, a man signalled that he wanted to speak to me. Climbing on the wing he shouted as best he could against the slipstream that the aircraft had been reallotted to Bognor. Next day, a

An Auster light aircraft, used as airborne observation platforms in Normandy.

White Waltham No.1 Ferry Pool in late 1945 after closure of Hamble and Cosford Women's Ferry Pools.

Sunday, No. 1 Ferry Pool turned out a strong team to move the whole GSU. I don't know how many aircraft there were, but we spent the whole day at it, leaving White Waltham at eight forty-five in the morning and getting back, without even a stop for lunch, after ten o'clock that night.

From Bognor an ATA Anson took us back to Redhill after each trip – a half-hour flight – to pick up another aircraft. One of the No. 1 Pool pilots made seven trips, five in Spitfires, one in a Typhoon and one in an Auster. The Austers would have been for No.661 AOP Squadron who were in Normandy supporting the Canadian Army. Between each trip we had to wait until enough pilots had arrived to fill the Anson. There must, I thought as I got tired and irritable, be an easier way of putting in two and a half hours flying! Frankie Francis, our Commanding Officer who was flying one of the taxi Ansons, put in seven and a half hours flying and probably some twenty landings – the majority without stopping engines. His logbook showed simply 'White Waltham – Redhill etc.' with the total time, a most unusual entry as normally we were punctilious when filling in our logbooks. Perhaps this reflected an unusual and thoroughly exhausting day. My share in this amounted to three Typhoons, a Spitfire XI, a Hurricane and an Auster, a total of only 2 hrs 20 minutes flying.

CHAPTER 20

ATA CLOSES – MY NEXT JOB

During November 1945 we were told that ATA would close at the end of the month and by the end of that year the war, had virtually been forgotten in the flurry of preparation for the brave new world. As I had no private income it was essential that I lost no time in getting a job. I had kept my commercial 'B' licence current throughout the war and this now listed ten types of public transport aircraft including the Oxford, Anson, Mosquito and Lancaster, and my licence also entitled me to fly all types of landplane for aerial work and private flying. I also had a navigator's licence, the training for which ATA had paid. To start with therefore I wrote round to airlines who were advertising for pilots. For the most part they interviewed me, mostly, I felt out of curiosity, before thinking up a reason for not taking me on.

Amongst the jobs I applied for was one as an Operations Officer with the Ministry of Civil Aviation, although I had no idea what an operations officer did and in any case, I was unaware that they had never employed a female in this post up till then. Meanwhile I continued looking round for a job, but nothing materialised, so when the Ministry came up with an offer I accepted it thankfully.

Whilst job-hunting I had moved to a bed-sitter in London. There was no question of affording a flat and the concept of flat-sharing, common as it is today, hadn't yet arrived. Searches for more agreeable accommodation led me to Wimbledon where I found a guest house in Somerset Road, adjacent to the All England Tennis Club grounds. Here for £10 a month I got breakfast and an evening meal but, better still, it accommodated half a dozen other inmates, for the most part of my own age. Two other of these had also been pilots, but in those immediate post-war days we didn't discuss wartime activities. It therefore was some time before I found out more about them. One had been shot down early in the war in a Whitley and another, who for many years remained a good friend, had flown Hurricanes in North Africa and the Far East. The atmosphere there was a happy one and at weekends we would walk

...enes from the closing pageant at White Waltham. Below is the Liberator that I was assigned to ...ing in for the occasion.

together on the common, play squash at the Wimbledon Squash Club in Worple Road, where I became a member. I was the only one with a car and petrol permitting, we drove to such places as Kew Gardens where the entrance fee was as far as I remember, either a penny or twopence.

I joined the Ministry of Civil Aviation (MCA) on 18th February 1946 in Inveresk House in the Strand. My Deputy Director in the Directorate of Operations was Air Commodore Murray, who was completely non-plussed at having a woman posted to his Deputy Directorate. Instead of sending me to one of the ops branches, he set me up as his personal assistant, something the 'old hands' – the Heads of Ops branches were men who had remained in jobs connected with civil aviation during the war – were not at all happy about. Shortly after I arrived it was in this capacity that I went to Dublin with nebulous duties as part of the British Delegation to the PICAO Conference, called to discuss facilities for post-war North Atlantic routes. We were there for three weeks and on 17th March a reception was laid on by Irish Prime Minister Eamon de Valera, of whom I have a photograph which includes myself and others of our team.

Reception at President's House Dublin, 7/3/46, Eamon deValera is in the bow tie.

Whilst I was away more complaints about my status in the Directorate had been raised. Senior Operations Officers said that Operations Officers should not be used as Personal Assistants. Thus shortly afterwards I was posted to a branch called C.Ops.5 whose duties were to co-ordinate Air Traffic Control, Telecommunication and Met. facilities which were to be installed at the airfields now being opened up for civil use. This provided scope for many outside visits and a further benefit of the job was that MCA had its own fleet of aircraft based at Gatwick, then a grass airfield. These comprised an Auster, a Proctor and an Anson XIX which, as a licensed pilot, I was allowed to use for duty visits. Soon after my posting I spent a weekend at Gatwick being checked out, first on the Proctor and later on the Anson. Flights I made in the Proctor included one taking senior operations staff to Turnhouse, Perth and Errol. I also made one in an American Expeditor carrying a party of six Americans from Hendon to Manston, Hurn, St. Eval and back to London Airport before returning to Hendon.

As I got used to the job I found myself chairing meetings of ATC, Tels and Met staff at airfields which, during the war, had been run by the RAF. We would assemble in the control tower and argue about the allocation of accommodation. The top floor inevitably went to ATC, the next one down to Tels and the ground floor to Met, who in those days drew up and interpreted their own charts from data supplied to them. The sticking point was always the allocation of rest rooms, as a common rest room for all three branches was said to be unthinkable. In August, by way of a holiday, I flew a load of UNRA stores to Athens. These days it is difficult to imagine how ignorant a pilot could have been. My only overseas flights had been the odd ATA ferry flight to the continent and I knew nothing of such things as the effect of high temperature on performance or on fuel consumption. I left with a flight engineer from Croydon in Anson G-AHKI. The only radio we had was an ineffective HF/RT set which even in the circuit was difficult to use. Our first refuelling stop was at Le Bourget, the next at Marseilles where BOAC had a base and at a price, would look after refuelling and any necessary maintenance; here we stayed the night. Our next stop was at Bari where the RAF refuelled us, found us accommodation, supplied transport to an hotel on the sea front and collected us next morning for our final leg to

Athens. This was another BOAC station and we were met by Wing Commander Mills who, after being somewhat taken aback by the arrival of a female pilot, arranged for the stores to be unloaded and then fixed us with luxurious accommodation in the Grande Bretaigne Hotel. We took a day off before returning to England, this time with a load of grapes.

I had been with MCA for around a year when I answered an advertisement for a job as a government test pilot at either RAE Farnborough or A&AEE Boscombe Down. Acknowledgement of the application was addressed to E.L. Curtis Esq – so clearly, in spite of many clues, they hadn't got the message that I was female. I was summoned to an interview at Farnborough at 11 am on 21st January 1947, and they wrote that "travelling expenses not exceeding 3rd class return railway fare" would be refunded to me on arrival. Outside the board room an attendant informed me, as I already knew, that this was a board for test pilots. When he returned to the board room a roar of laughter went up, but presumably they had no option other than to call me in, so the interview proceeded. There were at the time many ex-service pilots looking for jobs so I was surprised to learn in due course that although they were not taking me on I was in first place on the waiting list. Returning to MCA, therefore, I thought no more about it.

In August that year I came back from holiday in Greece to find a telegram awaiting me at my digs in Somerset Road which said that if I was still interested I should ring Mr Marsden at Boscombe with a view to attending for a test flight. This was arranged for 15th August and it was at Boscombe that day that I met for the first time arguably the most experienced test pilot of all time, Group Captain H.A 'Bruin' Purvis.

In 1924 Purvis had entered Cranwell as a King's Cadet. In 1936 after various postings he joined the Engine Development Flight at RAE Farnborough where one of his first jobs was to deliver the DH Comet, which eventually won the England to Australia race in 1934, to the experimental station at Martlesham. During the flight both engines stopped, but he landed it undercarriage down in a cornfield. He remained in charge of the engine development flight until December 1939 and for the work was awarded his first AFC. The war saw Bruin, now a squadron leader, taking part in association with Vickers in trials of

Charges to pay

RECEIVED

At From

By

POST OFFICE

+ 2 19 2131 A AND A EE

EST 5 B 2 ONE +

No.

OFFICE STAMP

Yerds.

TSA 340 5.12 OHMS MINISTRY OF SUPPLY 43/40

MISS E L CURTIS 2 SOMERSET RD WIMBLEDON SW 19

= IF STILL INTERESTED IN TEST PILOT APPOINTMENT

REQUEST YOU TELEPHONE AMESBURY 2131 (MR MARSDEN)

WITH A VIEW TO ATTENDING FOR A TEST AT A AND A EE

BOSCOMBE DOWN = EST 5 B 2 SFLYMIN LONDON +

For free repetition of doubtful words telephone "TELEGRAMS ENQUIRY" or call, with this form
at office of delivery. Other enquiries should be accompanied by this form, and, if possible, the envelope. B or C

The telegram inviting me for a test flight at Boscombe.

Wellington P2518 which had fitted under its wings a 48 ft diameter ring and generator unit designed for exploding German mines. For his part in these tests he was awarded a DFC. His next two years were spent in the States as a member of the British Air Commission. When he returned in May 1942 he was posted to A&AEE Boscombe Down as Officer Commanding 'B' performance test squadron, where he remained until 1945. He had by now risen to the rank of Group Captain purely on the grounds of his flying and the time had now come for him to 'fly a desk.' Administration, however, was not his thing and, seeing for himself no future in the RAF, he resigned in June 1946 after twenty-two years flying.

In the meantime, a requirement had arisen at Boscombe for a new flight to test the civil aircraft coming into use with airlines. Bruin was offered and accepted the job of Chief Test Pilot in the new Civil Aircraft Test Section (CATS) and remained there until 1963 when he retired.

This was how I first came to meet him in August 1947. On arrival at Boscombe Down for a flight test I was horrified to find that this was to be on an Avro Tudor, which looked to me far more intimidating than the bombers I had flown during the war. We climbed aboard but luckily the aircraft was found to be unserviceable, so we climbed out again and into a Vickers Viking. I have no recollections of the flight except that I remember thoroughly enjoying it. It was at least ten days later that I got news of the result of the test. On the 26th I got a letter from Bruin which included the following:

"Following your visit we were quite satisfied that you would make a success of the job here and that the combination of flying and technical work is something for which you are well qualified."

He continued: "We have written to the Ministry of Supply saying we would consider you suitable for the post and it is now for the Establishment people to make an official approach to you. I am bound to tell you that they may hedge at employing a woman for, as you may realise, Government Departments do not like to set a precedent."

TELEPHONE:
AMESBURY 3121
EXT - 5 & 118

OFFICERS' MESS
ROYAL AIR FORCE STATION
· BOSCOMBE DOWN
AMESBURY, WILTS

26th Aug. 1947.

Dear Miss Curtis,

Thank you for your letter of the 16th of August. I must say that following your visit we were quite satisfied that you would make a success of the job here and that the combination of flying and technical work is something for which you are well qualified.

The official processes are now at work. We have written to the Ministry of Supply saying that we consider you suitable for the post, and it is now for the Establishment's people there to make an official approach to you. I am bound to tell you that they may hedge at employing a woman for, as you yourself realise, Government Departments do not like to set a precedent. I hope that everything will turn out alright.

Yours sincerely,

JCKS/KG.

I had a further letter from him in October saying: "I know how disappointed you must feel about the test business. There is going to be another advertisement in the next few weeks and if I were you I would apply. If we can say after a second advertisement that there is no other person with your qualifications and experience we can press ACS(A) to reverse the decision."

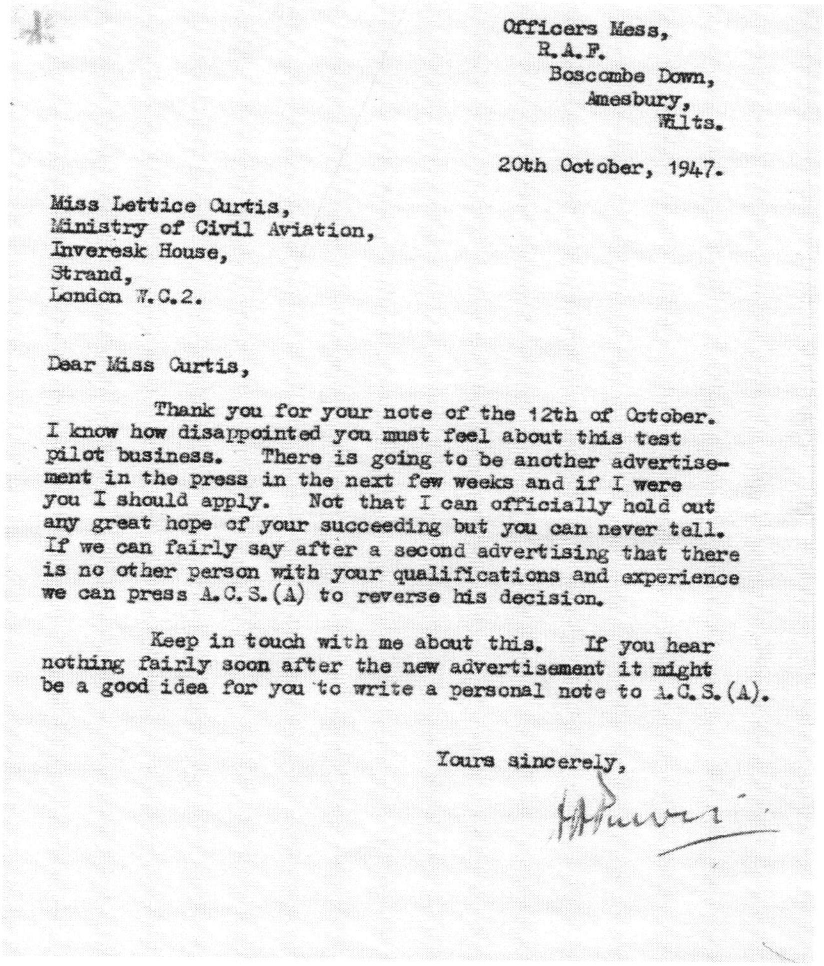

Officers Mess,
R.A.F.
Boscombe Down,
Amesbury,
Wilts.

20th October, 1947.

Miss Lettice Curtis,
Ministry of Civil Aviation,
Inveresk House,
Strand,
London W.C.2.

Dear Miss Curtis,

Thank you for your note of the 12th of October. I know how disappointed you must feel about this test pilot business. There is going to be another advertisement in the press in the next few weeks and if I were you I should apply. Not that I can officially hold out any great hope of your succeeding but you can never tell. If we can fairly say after a second advertising that there is no other person with your qualifications and experience we can press A.C.S.(A) to reverse his decision.

Keep in touch with me about this. If you hear nothing fairly soon after the new advertisement it might be a good idea for you to write a personal note to A.C.S.(A).

Yours sincerely,

This was followed on 31st October by a letter from the Ministry of Supply Est.5B which said: "I am directed to inform you that previous experience as a test pilot is an essential requirement for the handling of aircraft at the Aircraft and Armament Experimental Establishment. In the circumstances it is regretted that your application must be regarded as unsuccessful."

A considerable amount of correspondence now followed with the Establishment Branch and with Air Marshal Sir Alex Coryton, who had charge of all test pilots, also with his deputy Air Vice Marshal E.J. Cuckney. On November 12th Establishments wrote to say that my name was being kept under review for consideration in the event of further vacancies for test pilots becoming available. In the meantime Bill Shipp, head of CATS in the Performance Division, pulled some strings to get me interviewed for the post as a Scientific Experimental Officer so that I could come and join them.

Gerard d'Erlanger, now Chairman of the new British European Airways, had written to Coryton asking for more information as to why I was not being allowed to take the job. The reply dated 29 December from the Air Marshal included: " . . . but due to the fact that she has no experience on prototypes, and the test work at Boscombe is for obvious reasons confined so far as is humanly possible to those qualified test pilots who have had operational experience in the type they are testing, we could not employ her at Boscombe. In the meantime she has been

Commodore Gerard d'Erlanger during his spell as head of the ATA.

offered a Senior Experimental Officer's post at either Boscombe or Farnborough. If she accepts that it will in no way affect her chances of ultimately going to Farnborough as a pilot for routine test work." As the civil aircraft coming to Boscombe would have been flown previously only by the firm's test pilots, one wonders where such pilots were going to be found.

I had by now decided to take a job offered at Boscombe as a flight test observer and had put in my resignation to the Ministry of Civil Aviation. On resigning I was interviewed by our Director, AVM Sir Conrad Collier, who had been posted to MCA as Controller, Technical and Operational Services, in which post he was responsible for the installation of Air Traffic Control, Navigational Aids and Telecommunications at the new Civil Airfields. He strongly recommended that I take the Boscombe job; perhaps he was disillusioned with his own post as he himself resigned in February 1948, even before I left.

My accepted leaving date was 31st March 1948, but before then I took on some flying for the American Civil Air Attaché, Livingston (Tony) Satterthwaite, who had been given a Spitfire by the British Government to fly whilst he was here. Before leaving I was taken out to lunch by Ted Heath, the future Prime Minister who was a wartime Army colleague of my brother-in-law Bill Murdock and who after the war, worked for a short time for the Ministry of Civil Aviation.

CHAPTER 21

THE AMERICAN SPITFIRE

Sir Peter Masefield, who a couple of years previously had been posted to Washington as British Civil Air Attaché, had been allowed to take with him a Proctor (G-AHGN). Tony, envious of this, sought permission from his government for an aircraft to use in Britain and Europe. The US Government, however, unwilling to ship an aircraft from the States for him, asked him to apply to the Air Ministry for a surplus Fairchild Argus. But Tony, unimpressed by the poor performance of this aircraft, asked instead for a war-surplus Spitfire.

On 14th April 1948 a letter was sent from the Embassy in London to the Department of State in Washington which included the following:

"I have the honour to report that the Ministry of Supply has made available to the Embassy for the use of the Civil Air Attaché a Vickers-Supermarine Spitfire Mk. XI. Spitfires are now obsolete as fighter aircraft in the RAF, having been replaced operationally by jets. Production of Spitfires has been discontinued. There are, and have been, therefore, many surplus Spitfires, and the one turned over to the Embassy presumably would either have been salvaged or pickled for future use. Mark XI Spitfires are photo-reconnaissance types, fitted with long-range tanks and have no guns or armour. The Embassy Spitfire has been registered under American registry by the Civil Aeronautics Administration. The number is N74138."

On leaving the RAF the aircraft went first to 33 Maintenance Unit at Lyneham, where military equipment was removed, and was then sent on to Vickers to be prepared for civil use. On 27th January 1948 the aircraft was ready for hand-over and Tony was asked to collect it from Southampton Eastleigh. Now an American aircraft, the Spitfire was to be held by the American Embassy Flight at Hendon, where informal arrangements had been made with RAF Hendon for servicing; Hendon then was where after hand-over, it was required to go.

The Embassy's Spitfire N74138

But Tony, although he already had use of an Embassy Harvard, did not feel happy about making his first flight in a Spitfire to Hendon which, even for those days, was a small airfield. Now Tony was a good friend of mine and in a rash moment, although I had flown only light aircraft since leaving the ATA over three years before, I volunteered to fly it to Hendon for him. Thus on a dreary January day we motored down to Eastleigh and, the presentation over, I had no option but to get in and start it up. No radio was fitted – the military one would have been removed at Lyneham – so it was a question of map-reading. Hendon at the time had two runways; one, 1,000 yards long, ran from north-east to south-west; the other from east to west was 800 yards long and the approach from the east was over a railway embankment. Arriving at Hendon I was more than a little relieved to find the "T" on the longer runway, nevertheless it was with great concentration that I made my approach and, in the event, managed a reasonable landing. Next day Air Marshal Sir John Boothman KBE, CB, DFC, AFC, who as A.C.A.S. Technical Requirements had been involved in the transfer of the aircraft to Satterthwaite, rang him at his office. He, it so happened, had been at Hendon when the aircraft arrived and was ringing to congratulate him on what he took to be his first Spitfire landing. Inevitably he was somewhat shaken to be told that the pilot had in fact been a woman.

But Tony was still not happy about taking the Spitfire in and out of Hendon, so when he wanted to fly I would take half a day's leave to take it initially to Bovingdon where there was a longer runway. It was not until 25th February that Tony made his first flight from there, after which I returned the aircraft to Hendon. But at the end of the month I was due to change my job in London for one at Boscombe Down. Ten days before the move I borrowed the Spit. and flew down to Boscombe to tie up loose ends. I have often wondered what people there thought about a junior future employee – and a woman at that – arriving for an interview in a Spitfire! On the 11th April I again took the Spit. to Bovingdon, where it must have gone unserviceable because my log book shows that I returned it to Hendon after a test flight on May 1st. It was 22nd May before Tony flew it again, this time from Hurn. He picked me up from Boscombe in the Harvard – in which for some reason I always took over the flying – and we flew back to Hendon to collect the Spit. At Hurn there were again serviceability problems and it was 9th June before we picked it up again and took it to Bovingdon, from where someone from Hendon had taken over flying it in and out. From Bovingdon we flew back in the Harvard to Thruxton, a club airfield close to Boscombe.

Whilst we were there we learnt that an Air Day was being arranged for 15th August 1948, which was to include a handicap race open to all types of aircraft. Air Racing first took place before WW1, but in 1914 aeroplanes, balloons and airships, with those who created and flew them, became part of the First World War. In 1921 serious air racing restarted and in the inter-war years many pilots who are now household names took part in them. It was not until 1949 that National Air Races, organised by the Royal Aero Club, restarted, but other races such as the one at Thruxton were organised before that. In another rash moment I suggested to Tony that he enter his Spitfire, to which he some-what surprisingly replied that if I raced the Spit. he would himself enter in the Harvard. Thus on 12th August Tony collected me from Boscombe and took me to Hendon to collect the Spitfire, which I flew back to Thruxton. But before racing the aircraft the engine would have to be thoroughly checked and the racing number painted on. I therefore sought permission from our A.O.C. Air Commodore 'Sam' Patch as we called him - later Air Chief Marshal Sir Hubert Patch CBE - to bring the Spitfire to Boscombe, where Rolls-Royce representatives had volunteered to check out the engine, and CATS engineers to service, help polish and paint on the race number. In those days aircraft were handicapped against full-throttle performance. On becoming a civil aircraft mercifully, the engine had been de-rated from +18 psi maximum boost to +12 psi, which with 2,850 rpm would have to be held for around half an hour. The Rolls Royce reps however told me that this should cause no problems. ATA recommended cruise was 2,000 rpm and zero boost so for me, racing was going to be something very different from what I was used to! The race was from Thruxton to Totland Bay in the Isle of Wight and back, and all other aircraft in the race were light aircraft types. On handicap therefore I had a 30-minute wait from when the first Auster took off until my turn came to be flagged away. As I waited on the start line I had to decide when to start the engine. If I started it too early it would overheat, if too late and it didn't start immediately, I would miss my starting time.

By the time I took off some light aircraft were already on the way back. Immediately after getting airborne I made a climbing turn to

R;
ck Rasmussen
iason Office),
LC,
ny
tterthwaite,
Mann
Chief Inspector)

2,000 feet so as to be above the rest of the field. Whilst still on the ground engine coolant temperature had reached the maximum and the needle remained at maximum throughout the flight – my only worry. A 180° turn round the marker at Totland Bay and I was on my way back. It was only after I dropped the nose to gain speed over the finishing line that I saw other aircraft below me; before landing I made a couple of circuits to cool the engine.

Also in the race was Bruin Purvis, Chief Test Pilot of the Civil Section in which I worked, in a Proctor he had entered with Sandy Powell, another test pilot. He told me afterwards that he had been convinced that he was winning and was not at all pleased when, within seconds of crossing the line, the Spitfire shot past him. One can only congratulate the handicappers! On the strength of this win Tony was asked to enter the Spitfire for the prestigious Lympne high-speed handicap race, which he did. Until the race, which was on 28th August, I was allowed to keep the Spitfire at Boscombe in the CATS hangar. Two days before the race I gave the Spitfire a short test flight and the following day flew it to Lympne, supported by 'Doc' Stuart who followed in his car. At Lympne the first person to meet me was Murray Payn, brother of my ATA friend Armstrong Payn. Surprised to see him, I asked him what he was doing here to which he replied, "I've married the (Lympne) Castle" which was a large house overlooking the channel. Doc and I booked into an hotel in Folkestone where we were joined by Tony and his wife for a happy evening.

The 1948 High Speed Handicap Air Race was run from the Cinque Ports Flying Club at Lympne. In those days aircraft firms would enter military types they were developing, hiring them for the day from the equivalent of the Ministry of Defence. The aircraft were raced by their test pilots. The course which included two very sharp turns, was over four circuits of a 20-mile course from Capel airship hangar at Folkestone Harbour pier, along the sea front to Hythe gas holder, and then back to Lympne. Participants in this race included Leslie Colquhoun in a Spitfire Mk.VIII Trainer, the winner of the race; John Cunningham and John Derry were in de Havilland Vampires; J.O. Matthews from Fairey's was in a Mk. 4 Firefly; W.J.G. Morgan was in a Spitfire Mk 24 and from Hawkers, T.S. Wade was in a Mk. I Hawker

Thruxton Air Race, 'Doc' Stuart comes out to tell me that I had won.

Fury. A Meteor VII had been entered by Bill Waterton but did not take part in the race. To me, ill-prepared and an amateur who had only flown a Spitfire at full power on one occasion on a there-and-back course, this was a daunting experience. On behalf of Tony as well as myself, I was seriously afraid of making a complete fool of myself. But it was too late to pull out now. At this time Lympne had no hard runway and the run was not all that long for Vampire jets, especially on grass. The wind was light and there was some indecision as to take-off direction. In the event we all started up and taxied to the west to take off towards the sea. Then at the last minute the Vampires, which were being given priority, requested take-off east-to-west so we all had to taxi to the other side of the field.

This was where my Spit put me at a disadvantage. The radiators on this model opened automatically when the coolant reached a speci-fied temperature and as no manual control was provided, remained open until the temperature dropped again. During the extended taxiing the radiator flaps had opened, increasing drag, and they remained open for the first three of the laps, the fourth lap showing an increase in speed of some seven mph. This increase if applied to the other three laps could with a very favourable handicap have won me the race – in spite of the fact that my turns could not compete with those of the professionals. As it was the honours went to Leslie Colquhoun in the Spitfire Trainer; John Cunningham, who came second, averaged, according to next day's press, 521 mph over the last three laps. I came fifth which could have been worse! Throughout the race Tony stood under the control tower keeping a check on the Spit and talking to celebrities which included

ELC in the Spitfire at the Lympne air-race.

Douglas Fairbanks Junior. We spent another night in Folkestone celebrating and next day I flew the Spitfire back to Hendon. This was the last time I flew it as Tony had been posted back to the Department of State in Washington. Before he went we spent many hours discussing the possibilities of flying the Spit to America, but under the terms of the gift, the aircraft could not it appeared be domiciled outside the UK. Tony Satterthwaite in due course became First Secretary in the U.S. Embassy in Copenhagen where on one occasion I had a very happy holiday. In October 1959 he was killed in a helicopter accident whilst visiting his 'parish' in Greenland. With his death, Great Britain lost one of America's most ardent Anglophiles.

After the race, in spite of my unspectacular performance, the Royal Aero Club awarded me an FAI Class C certificate for a British Women's National Record, for achieving a speed of 313.208 miles an hour over a 100 kilometre closed circuit course in a Vickers-Supermarine Spitfire XI. The certificate is signed by Lord Brabazon of Tara, President of the Royal Aero Club of Britain. Later George

Lindgren, Parliamentary Secretary to the Ministry of Aviation, who had been watching the race, invited me to lunch in the House of Commons where, I recall, the main course was whale meat!

On the weekend of 31st July, August 1949, racing started up again at Birmingham - Elmdon, with the first of the post-war National Air Races. On the Saturday, three heats followed by a final was run for the Kings Cup, a race confined to British pilots flying British-built aircraft for which there were thirty six entries. Also run was the high-speed race for the Kemsley Trophy from which Tom Brooke-Smith who had entered a Short Sturgeon, retired so that in a Short Sealand, he could compete in the final of the Kings Cup. There were seven entries for the high speed Kemsley Trophy race which was won by Neville Duke in the P.1040 -forerunner of the Harrier - at 508mph, John Cunningham in a Vampire coming second at 470mph.

For Sunday, five events were scheduled. These included the Grosvener Challenge Cup for aircraft ineligible for the Kings Cup and weighing less than 2000kg. The Siddeley Challenge Trophy for members of the Association of British Aero Clubs and the Norton Griffiths Challenge Trophy, for aircraft weighing between 2000kg and 3850kg. The Air League Challenge Cup was open to aircraft of any nationality with a maximum speed of more than 250mph. This was won by P.G.Lawrence in the Blackburn Firebrand. For the SBAC Challenge Cup which was announced as the world's fastest race, there were only three starters. John Derry in the DH.108, John Cunningham in a Vampire, and 'Wimpy' Wade in the P.1040 who was declared the winner at 510mph, and who recorded the fastest lap at 562mph.

Boscombe Down was well represented in the Kings Cup in which both Bruin Purvis and 'Doc' Stuart had entered Proctors. Amongst other entrants was Captain Peter Townsend in a Miles Whitney Straight who had been entered by entered by Princess Margaret. None of these however qualified for the final. On the Sunday however Bruin in his Proctor took part in the Norton Griffiths race and came in third. I too took part in the Norton Griffiths in 'Doc' Stuart's Proctor, ending in fifth place with an Aurocrat which the judge declared to be the first dead heat in 25 years! In Boscombe's Ercoupe - which as it was not a government aircraft I was allowed to fly - I took part in the Grosvener

ELC in the Ercoupe at Elmdon in 1949.

Trophy which was for aircraft weighing less that 2000kg. On handicap I started near the front but still ended in 11th place. However at 112.5 mph I won £20 for the fastest aircraft weighing less than 2000kg, something strongly disputed by Group Captain Mole in his Benes-Mraz-Bibi, who claimed that the Ercoupe was over weight and insisted that it was put on the scales before the prize was awarded!

In April 1950 I bought my own aircraft, two-seater Wicko G-AFJB, buying it from my wartime friend Philippa Bennett. In the autumn of 1941 we had both been amongst the women pilots at Hatfield who were sent to Hamble to start the second all-woman ferry pool. Later, when it was decided that previously all male ferry pools should take in women, I moved to one of the 'mixed' ferry pools. Phil however remained at Hamble, staying there for the rest of the war as one of their stalwarts and senior pilots. When ATA closed Phil who had a house in Hamble, set up an air charter company P.M.Bennett Ltd, using amongst other aircraft, Wicko G-AFJB for her taxi work. Wickos had been built by Geoffrey Wickner, an Australian who himself was a cousin of Edgar Wikner Percival founder of the Percival Aircraft Company. He arrived in England in 1934 and set up a company Foster Wikner Aircraft for which in 1936, a production line was set up at Southampton Eastleigh to build Wickos. His second aircraft, Wicko G-AEZZ, although not shown as an entrant in British Racing and Record Breaking Aircraft, was said to have been entered for the 1936 Kings Cup. When war broke out production of his aircraft could not be continued, and Wickner himself joined ATA. G-AFJB, which in 1938 had been sold to the Midland Aero Club was amongst those put to use with the ATA as a taxi aircraft. When war ended, surviving Wickos were returned to Eastleigh and G-AFJB was bought by Philippa for use by her charter company. But in 1950 the Wicko, which was only a two seater was put up for sale, and this was the point at which I bought it. Thus on April 5 1950 I collected it from Eastleigh and took it to Boscombe Down where I had been given permission by the AOC to keep it.

With the air race season starting, it was not long before I decided to enter it for air races and in August that year, I entered it for the Goodyear Trophy race at Wolverhampton. This was the first time a Wicko had been raced since before the war when it was owned by Wikner, and many modifications had been made. The handicappers however judged it on its pre-war performance estimating that it was capable of 130mph, some 10mph more than the aircraft could now achieve. The result was that the handicap was so excessive that I retired after the first lap. Back at Boscombe however, I again entered it for the Thruxton-Isle of Wight race which I had last entered in the Spitfire.

My two-seat Wicko G-AFJB

This time 'Doc' Stuart came with me as my navigator. The dual navigation however was not a success and no doubt, the extra weight didn't help either! Amongst other races I took part in later were the Daily Express races of 1950, 1951 and 1952 but in none of these was I amongst the winners. Contributing to this was the fact that I had no time to carry out practice runs over the course which particularly in the Hurn to Herne Bay race, was unfamiliar. The only time the Wicko won a prize was in July 1951 when I lent it to 'Doc' for the Bristol air race. Although he did not win, he was delighted to come back with a prize! For every race entered you were liable to be given a new race number which had to be painted on the fin. Luckily our CATS ground staff kindly helped me out with this specialist task.

Daily Express Air Race, Hurn 28/9/50. ELC in Wicko and George Miles in an Aerovan.

ELC with Peggy Grace at Shoreham for the Daily Express Air Race in August 1952.

CHAPTER 22

THE AEROPLANE AND ARMAMENT EXPERIMENTAL ESTABLISHMENT (A. & A.E.E.) BOSCOMBE DOWN

When I arrived at Boscombe Down on 1st April 1948, the first thing I had to do was to find somewhere to live. A&AEE had a hostel in Manor Road, Salisbury and it was here that I booked in for a bed. The next two days were spent looking for more permanent accommodation. I settled for a room with breakfast and evening meal at 41 Hulse Road, Salisbury with a family named Gorringe. I remained there until when, five years later, I left Boscombe. The house was on the River Avon, upstream of a railway bridge. I still have a cup marked 'S.R' – Southern Railway – which I picked up from the river where, locals reckoned, things were often thrown out of train windows by passengers approaching the station. I still had my small Lancia Augusta so transport to and from Amesbury was no problem. At the RAF Mess in days before WAAF had moved in, I was the first female to become a Mess member. At A&AEE Boscombe Down there were four military test Squadrons; 'A' Squadron tested fighters, 'B' Squadron bombers, 'C' Squadron was a Royal Navy Squadron which tested RN aircraft, and later when the Airborne Forces Experimental Establishment moved to Boscombe from Beaulieu, 'D' Squadron was formed to deal with helicopters.

There was also the Civil Aircraft Test Squadron (CATS) that carried out clearance tests on civil airliners and this was the squadron I was joining. Technical head of CATS was J.C.K. Shipp, and the chief civil test pilot was Group Captain 'Bruin' Purvis who as already stated, had retired from the RAF to take this job. It was he who, as mentioned in a previous chapter, had flight-tested me and been brave enough to say that he would be happy to take me on as one of his test pilots. Bruin's second in command was 'Doc' Stuart, a wartime Fleet Air Arm pilot of some distinction, who also became a good friend.

Boscombe was still a grass airfield and I particularly remember the short northerly uphill run pointing towards the hangars, which were hit during the war by an ATA Liberator that failed to take off. Because the pilot was very experienced, no single reason could be found for the accident, but those were early days for nose-wheeled aircraft and, looking back, it seems inevitable that the short grass uphill run was in fact too short for this type of aircraft to become airborne. It was whilst I was at Boscombe that the first hard runway was built.

The job I had been taken on for was to fly as an observer in test aircraft, recording manually the basic instruments from which aircraft performance was accessed. I was also responsible for writing up the post-flight report. In my first months with CATS, routine trials were being carried out on Tudor 1s G-AGRI and G-AGRD. My first flight was on April 5th, when we measured fuel consumptions in Tudor G-AGRI. The Tudor 1, Britain's first post-war airliner, had been ordered for BOAC to use on the Atlantic, but it had insufficient range and BOAC took on instead the American Constellation. The concentration on fuel consumptions was allied to BOAC's rejection of the Tudor I for the Atlantic. Tudor 2 VX202 came to Boscombe in the summer of 1948, as did Tudors 7 and 8 later in the year.

The Tudor 4 had been adapted for use by British South American Airways and after the unexplained loss of Star Tiger, which disappeared between the Azores and Bermuda in January 1948, all Tudor 4s were grounded. As part of the investigation into the reason for the accident, Tudor 4 Star Leopard was sent to Boscombe for extended tests. The first tests involved fuel consumptions to see whether it could have run out of fuel. Aircraft performance was also measured in various failed engine conditions with both one or even two engines out. However, no explanation was found for the loss of Star Tiger. Later the loss was attributed to the aircraft having got lost and running out of fuel for at that time navigation was based solely on astro-navigation.

In July 1948 tests started at Boscombe on Hermes II G-AGUB. This was a lengthened version of the Hermes 1, which had crashed at Radlett on its first flight in December 1945. It was September 1947 before the modified Mark II flew. Although American airliners were now being fitted with nose-wheels, the Hermes II still had a tail wheel and as a result of the Mk.1 disaster, the first tests inevitably consisted of stability measurements. In May 1949 Hermes IV G-AKFP, the first British airliner to be fitted with a nose-wheel, came to Boscombe for full clearance. The Ministry of Supply had called for the test programme to cover take-off and landing distances, rates of climb in various conditions, engine cooling and fuel consumptions. The results had to be submitted to Cabinet level by 31st May to enable BOAC to make a route analysis. Tests were initially to be carried out at a maximum take-off weight of 82,000 lb, later raised to 86,000 lb, and at a maximum landing weight of 75,000 lb. It was at the higher weight that the aircraft was taken to Khartoum and Nairobi for tropical and higher altitude tests in which I played a full part. Out of 25 Hermes IVs ordered by BOAC, 20 were eventually accepted, but G-AKFP was one of those rejected for being over weight.

During April 1949 Ambassador G-AGUR returned to Boscombe at the request of the Ministry of Supply for a further handling assessment after modifications had been made to deal with severe shaking in the rear fuselage. I see that I spent no less than 28 hours in this aircraft during the trials so the total hours spent on Ambassador tests must have been significantly more. Although A&AEE were still not-completely happy with it, it must have been deemed acceptable to the Ministry as it went into service at least for a time with BEA as an Elizabethan.

ermes IV -AKFP at hartoum.

One of the trials carried out around this time in which technical staff were allowed to join, even if they had little part to play, was a Gust Research programme for which Viking VL226 was used. This involved four or five day trips when suitable weather conditions were forecast, to measure the size of super-cooled water droplets which it was thought, made a contribution to the understanding of aircraft icing. The first trip in which I was included came in December 1948 with Bruin the pilot, when we went via Istres and Rome to Malta where we spent two nights in the RAF transit mess. In Malta my brother Robert, a Royal Marine Commando, was at the time in charge of the Royal Navy camp at Ghajn Tuffieh. At the same time a cousin, General Revell-Smith was the Governor General. On the first night my brother joined us in the Mess and on the second, I was invited to dinner in Government House. As I had no responsibilities in respect of Gust Research it was for me a happy holiday. In the five years I was at Boscombe I stopped in Malta on one test or another no less than seven times. On one of the trips I was taken with our crew down to the 'gut' where I never worked out why, whilst sitting alone while the men were at the bar, the ladies of the house came and sat on either side of me! On a later visit yet another cousin, Major General 'Bill' Heath, was now Governor General so I again dined at Government House, to be served by the same waiter as on my previous visit.

On 28th May 1948 Brian Bastable, another of the civil test pilots, was killed with Beryl Edmonds, a young scientific officer. Beryl was the daughter of the Bristol Engines representative and was on board as observer whilst flight-testing Marathon prototype G-AGPD. The Marathon, a high winged aircraft with four Gipsy Queen engines built by Miles was designed for use as a feeder aircraft carrying up to 20 passengers. As such it had been ordered by both BEA and BOAC, with BOAC planning to use it with a smaller number of passengers in East Africa. The prototype had three fins, the outboard ones of which were adjustable to help it was thought, with directional control in the event of engine failure on take-off. On this flight however problems arising with the adjustment resulted in a catastrophic structural failure. After this Miles, who were already in financial difficulties, were taken over by Handley Page, who pressed on with a redesign.

The second Marathon, G-AILH, came in due course to CATS to complete tests with a redesigned tail which now incorporated two instead of three fixed fins. British European Airways, not happy with the aircraft which they had planned to use to replace their DH.89 Rapides, had already passed on some of their Marathon order to the RAF. BOAC still hoped to use it in East Africa, but first needed performance figures for operating under hot and high conditions. Thus the task fell to CATS to assess its performance at Khartoum and Nairobi.

The A&AEE retained during the summer months a unit at RAF Khartoum and it was here that aircraft, both military and civil, were attached for tropical trials. On 7 November 1949 – unusually late in the year for such trials to start – Marathon G-AILH left Boscombe for Khartoum. To meet user requirements the weight of the production aircraft had been raised from 16,500 lb to 18,000 lb and, to get a Certificate of Airworthiness, performance data was called for at this weight. The amount of fuel carried was such that maximum stage lengths were only some 450 miles. This made the trip to Khartoum, as far as I was concerned, the most memorable of a number I was later involved in in the Hermes, Viscount and – after I joined Fairey's – the

Fairey Gannet. The Marathon crew consisted of pilot Doc Stuart, John Mills 'key-bashing' radio operator, myself responsible for collecting the necessary performance data and a representative from Handley Page who had now taken over the Miles factory. A maintenance crew of five also came with us. Allowing for daily inspections carried out by our ground crew each morning, and the maximum range of some 400 miles, it took us four days and nine intermediate stops to reach Khartoum. Our first refuelling stop was at Bordeaux during the day and we spent our first night at Nice. The next day, after refuelling at Rome, we continued to Malta where we spent our second night. We refuelled again at Benina and at El Adem where we bathed in the Mediterranean from the Officers Club at Tobruk while the engineers worked on some minor unserviceability. After walking on the pale and inviting sands, we were told that they harboured fish with spikes sufficiently poisonous to put one's life at risk.

The flight along the North African coast such a short time after WW2 was particularly evocative as the names of El Adem, Tobruk, Mersa Matruh and Sidi Barrani – which we passed at low level – were daily in the news and ships sunk in the war could be seen clearly through the water. It was then on to Cairo where we night-stopped in the Heliopolis Hotel. Next day, following the Nile to Luxor and Wadi Halfa, we finished with a night landing at Khartoum.

The Tropical Experimental Unit (TEU) was headed by a Squadron Leader seconded from Boscombe. Civilian photographers, whose main task was to deal with the automatic observer cameras and develop the yards of film used on each flight, took it in turn to man the unit during the trials season. TEU had its own sleeping quarters consisting of wooden huts outside the main RAF Guard Room – the latter being a large arched gatehouse outside of which there was a huge 'HALT' sign scrawled in Arabic across the road. Crews fed in RAF Messes, Officers' or Sergeants', according to rank. The Trials team were issued with bicycles to get around the camp and one lady's bike was thoughtfully provided for me, but when this got a puncture – as happened all too frequently – I had to use one with a bar and got quite adept when bicycling in a skirt at lifting my leg over the bar frontwise as did the Sudanese in their ankle-length jalabiyas.

A very special feature of the Transit Mess was a native named Osman who, every evening before dinner, laid out his wares of wood, hide, ivory and crocodile skin on the Mess veranda. I still have a collection of small ivory animals of every size and shape, bought on various trips to Khartoum. Bargaining with Osman was a way of life at the camp. Osman never forgot a face and would recognise people who had not passed through for years; he was reputed to be very wealthy. This was the first of several visits I made to Khartoum and I have many happy memories of the town; it was laid out by Lord Kitchener in 1898 and the European buildings, including the Governor's Palace, the University, Grand Hotel and the Sudan Club all overlooked the Blue Nile. On the western outskirts of the town the Blue Nile joins the White Nile and, just above the confluence, a bridge connects Khartoum with the native village of Omdurman, said at the time to be the largest native village in Africa. Our main recreation when not flying was to visit the Sudan Club where there was a large swimming pool – swimming in the Nile was not recommended – and where tea was served with fresh milk. This particular luxury owed its existence to the Kifouri family who against all odds, kept a herd of cows in North Khartoum. These were milked three times a day and the milk was delivered early each morning for storage in domestic fridges. As there was no grass, vast quantities of greenstuff had to be brought in daily to feed the cows.

Perhaps the most notable feature of life in Khartoum was the lack of water-borne sanitation, said to be only available in the Governor's Palace and the Grand Hotel. For the rest it was a matter of buckets; these were collected each night by camel carts termed 'lavender lizzies' which toured the streets at night, replacing used buckets with empties.

But back to the trials. Take-off and landing distances were measured at maximum all-up weight, the latter imposing severe strain on brakes and tyres. Low-level climb performance was measured with four, three and even two engines and, during all tests, temperatures were measured for comparison with those taken at home. Tests here took two and a half weeks to complete, after which we moved on to Nairobi.

The flight to Nairobi was another never-to-be-forgotten experience. We followed the Nile, refuelling at Malakal, after which we diverted to avoid flying over the Sudd a vast area of swamp, more inhospitable even than the desert if you came down. We refuelled at Juba and continued to Kisumo where we spent another night. At Nairobi we landed at the old civil airport, Eastleigh, which had murrem runways and was at 5,280 feet above sea level. ('Murrem' is a clayey iron-based natural material found locally, much used for roads, tracks or runways cut into the bush.) Here take-off and landing distances were measured, as was climb and level flight performance. After five days of tests we were ready to return to Khartoum en route to the UK. This time we got special permission from the British Authorities to night-stop at Juba. It was nearly dark when we arrived but an RAF Air Traffic Control Officer insisted in driving me round the airfield to see lions which, however, failed to appear. Next day we saw them from the air as well as elephant herds on the move.

We arrived back in Khartoum on 3rd December, expecting to be on our way home in a couple of days, but this was not to be. During a pre-flight inspection cracks were found in the tailplane and the aircraft was grounded. In due course orders came from home for the tailplane to be flown home in a Hastings for inspection, leaving us with nothing to do. The wind had gone round to the north signifying winter, and bathing was out. We bicycled to the outskirts of the town where road faded into desert and to what was then an excellent zoo where animals had minimum restrictions. There was a sailing club on the Blue Nile, but at this time of year one could get swept down to the confluence with the White Nile. Evenings were cold and one night when we decided to dine at the Grand Hotel we were told that à la carte was only served outside, so we collected all the braziers together round our table and dined in our overcoats.

Having been invited by Osman to visit Omdurman we hired a car and drove there, passing Madhi's tomb on the site of the famous battle. In the mud-walled village we took coffee with Osman's friends, and afterwards watched native craftsmen beating out, amongst other things, ceremonial swords for desert tribes and making billiard balls on foot-operated lathes. With thoughts of Christmas approaching, Khartoum was now rapidly losing its charms. It was nearly two weeks before the tailplane returned with instructions that the aircraft was to be flown home with minimum crew – which amounted to pilot and radio operator – and that I was to come home in a BOAC flying boat.

I flew home in Solent G-AHIM, which left at five o'clock on Sunday afternoon and, whilst waiting for it to arrive, I was allowed out in the Shell launch which swept the landing area. The Solent carried 34 passengers on two decks, on the upper one of which there was a cocktail lounge. Around midnight we were disembarked at Alexandria to watch an Arab doing conjuring tricks whilst the aircraft was refuelled. After a further six hours we reached Augusta in Sicily, where we were sent to an hotel overlooking the sea for a wash and breakfast. On the last leg in clear blue weather, our unpressurised aircraft passed just above the snow-capped peaks of the Alps Maritime and we finally landed in Southampton Water on 18th December. Would that flying could still be like this! The Marathon spent Christmas en route, arriving home on 27th December. Regretfully the measurements taken on these trials led to cancellation of BOAC's order, thirty going instead to the RAF as navigation trainers.

On 27th January 1952, in the early hours of Sunday morning, a Convair B-36, which had just completed a non-stop flight of over 51 hours from Carswell Air Force Base in Texas, landed at Boscombe Down some hundred yards short of the start of 06 runway. The Soviet blockade of Berlin had led to the decision to base bombers of the US Strategic Air Command (SAC) in Britain. The B-36, however, required runways both longer and stronger than those used by Britain's wartime bombers. Three new airfields, Marham, Lakenheath and Sculthorpe, were therefore being built to meet the new runway requirements. The decision to use these airfields was later revised when it was decided that they were in danger of sneak attacks by the Russians from across the North Sea. They were therefore replaced by enlarging the more westerly airfields of Upper Heyford, Brize Norton and Fairford.

The first ten engined – "six burnin', four turnin'" – B-36s to make the non-stop flight from Texas had arrived at the USAAF base at Lakenheath some ten days earlier. The one scheduled for Boscombe, where a hard runway had recently been built, was one of a second group making a non-stop training flight from Texas to the UK. In 1952 Boscombe Down airfield would have been equipped with VHF direction-finding and Drem lighting, the standard approach aids at a time when radar was reserved for front line operational stations.

At Boscombe the Air Officer Commanding was Air Commodore A.W.E. McDonald – later Air Marshal Sir Arthur McDonald KCB AFC – and he had acquired from the Telecommunications Research Establishment (TRE) at Malvern, a radar which tracked direction, but not height. The lighting would have consisted of an arc of lead-in lights extending some 2,000 yards from the airfield, plus 'funnel' lights set on either side of the extended runway centreline which started wide apart and narrowed as they approached the runway threshold. In the USA, we were told, runways were longer and approach lights were not used. Approach lights, therefore, were something the crew would not have been familiar with. The landing took place during a period of heavy frost when the ground was frozen hard – the reason why the aircraft was virtually undamaged even after landing in a field.

The arrival of the B-36 was a highly classified movement, so those of us working at the station knew nothing of its impending arrival. It was not till the following morning, when the aircraft was clearly visible from the Salisbury-Amesbury road, that unofficial stories about its arrival began to appear. One of these came from a senior member of the A&AEE technical staff who, on returning from a night out in Salisbury, saw the aircraft beside the Salisbury-Amesbury road; he got out of his car

The unfortunate B-36.

Another view of the B-36

and said to a crew member who was now walking about outside the aircraft: "If you want the airfield it's a mile down the line", then got back into his car and drove on. Another story going round was about the chap manning a VHF D/F Hut near the end of the runway who rang the control tower where the top brass were gathered, to report that there was an aircraft outside his hut.

"We haven't time to talk to you," he was told. "We are awaiting the arrival of a very important aircraft!"

Although I was at Boscombe at the time, it was not until 1994 that I decided to investigate the matter further as I felt that the story was worth writing up, and an article on my findings was published in Aeroplane Monthly in July that year. In order to learn more about what had happened I needed to start by talking to someone who had been in the control tower at the time. Amongst these would obviously have been Air Commodore Arthur McDonald, the station AOC. Now long retired from the RAF, I tracked him down in Lymington, got in touch with him and arranged a visit. Here I found that he recalled the incident – which had taken place over forty years previously – as if it had taken place yesterday and after our talk, he even got someone to drive him up to Amesbury to see again the place where the B-36 had landed. Amongst his memories was one of the conversations that took place between the Air Traffic Controller and the pilot, which went as follows:

Controller: "You are three miles from touchdown, slightly left of centreline."

Pilot: "OK."

Controller: "You are two miles from touchdown, on centreline."

Pilot: "I have landed." A slight pause, then: "My, isn't your field rough!"

Controller: "There's nothing wrong with our airfield, you're not on it. You are a quarter of a mile short of the touchdown position."

The aircraft was still showing on the radar, but the blip was now stationary. The bomber had finished up on the runway centreline, but between the Salisbury-Amesbury road and the airfield security fence, some 400 yards short of the threshold.

Also in the control tower was one Hewett. T. Wheless whom the USAAF had sent to liaise with the RAF. Assuming that the aircraft was seriously damaged he had immediately rung General McConnell at 7th Air Division to tell him that the crew were all right but that the B-36 was wrecked. McConnell then rang General J.B. Montgomery at 7th Air Command, the conversation, according to Wheless, going something like this:

Gen McConnell: "There is a farmer over here in England who is madder than hell with you."

Gen Montgomery: "What are you talking about?"

McConnell: "You landed a B-36 in the middle of a cornfield last night, and it's still there!"

Gen Montgomery: "That's not damn funny!"

McConnell: "I thought you might like the privilege of telling General LeMay about it."

A memo from McConnell to Montgomery three days later included the comment: "When you can land a B-36 aircraft in a hayfield three quarters of a mile from the runway, and when it can slide forwards, crossways and sideways past haystacks, farm buildings, through fences and across a primary highway including two ditches, with no damage on it except where a nosewheel fairing struck a fence post, all I can say is the Lord must be with us."

An additional story going round was that, before setting off, General LeMay had told the pilots that if anyone damaged their aircraft during the exercise, they could keep walking east and when their caps floated they could keep on walking. Although bad weather would no doubt have contributed to the misjudgement, it seems that mistaking the 'funnel' lights for runway lights was likely to have been the main cause. Retrieval of the bomber was arranged by the USAAF, who called in engineers working on the construction of Greenham Common airfield. They dug the topsoil away until the aircraft was standing on hard chalk, took the security fence down and towed the aircraft onto to the airfield. There, again according to Wheless, the only repair needed was a new bolt in the port undercarriage which was made by Boscombe engineers, and a new propeller to replace one damaged when the aircraft hit the haystack.

The night before the B-36 crew left, a memorable party was given for them in the Officers' Mess. When I mentioned this to Sir Arthur McDonald – who was more interested in boats than aeroplanes and was not a frequent user of the Officers' Mess bar – he said that if he had known about it, he would have stopped it going ahead!

CHAPTER 23

LINCOLN TO WOOMERA

In 1951, whilst writing up test results on various marks of Tudor, the Marathon and the Hermes, rumour reached the Civil Aviation Test Section that Lincoln RE258 was waiting at Farnborough to be delivered to the rocket range at Woomera. On the strength of this 'Doc' Stuart, our deputy chief test pilot, approached the Ministry of Supply offering to put together a civil crew from Boscombe to take it there. The volunteer crew from CATS which was in due course approved consisted of 'Pinkie' Pinkard, flight engineer, Ian Murdock, navigator, John Killykelly, 'key-bashing' radio operator – VHF was not yet in general use – 'Doc' Stuart, pilot, and myself, whom Doc had very broadmindedly agreed to take along as his second pilot.

As soon as approval was given, we set about planning the route and making preparations, which included a wide range of inoculations, visas and, most important of all, getting RAF pay books to enable us to draw local currency at our various points of call. We also applied to the Ministry of Supply for a tropical clothing allowance, which was refused on the grounds that, for this to be approved, you had to show you were going to spend at least ten days in the tropics.

The aircraft was duly brought to Boscombe by a Farnborough test pilot, where radio and compass checks were carried out. The aircraft was then weighed and generally prepared for the 11,000-mile journey which it was about to undertake. The starting date was fixed for 19th February and we were told we must start from Lyneham, where Customs facilities were available; we made arrangements therefore to night-stop there. Thus on the appointed day, after a number of flight tests, we piled ourselves and our luggage into the Lincoln, waved farewell to those we were leaving behind to face the English winter, and set off for Lyneham. Delayed by problems with one of the engines it was eight o'clock before we reached Lyneham; here we were offered a depressingly cold meal and then transported to Clyffe Pypard, where after some much needed drinks we retired to bed. My bed however was unaired and damp, and

The Lincoln that we took to Woomera.

in spite of adding strips of carpet to my bedclothes I still couldn't get warm. The night was a short one anyway as we were called at 05.30 to the accompaniment of pouring rain and gales.

Once back at the airfield we ate the inevitable fried 'flying' breakfast, cleared Customs and took off relying on a Met. forecast that the weather was better ahead. Happily this worked out to be correct as by 10,000 ft we were above the weather. After six hours' flying we reached a cold but sunny Malta. Here, as on a number of previous occasions, we stayed in the RAF Transit Mess at Luqa and, forgetting our short and sleepless night, went downtown to celebrate our first night out. We took off next morning at 9 o'clock for Cyprus where Air Commodore Alan Wheeler, AOC Cyprus, and his wife Barbara had come to meet us. The runway was short and, because he had landed with a small bounce, Doc's leg was pulled unmercifully, watchers telling him that he should have let his co-pilot do the landing! Doc and I stayed with the Wheelers where we were joined for supper by Air Commodore Chamberlain, AOC Transport Wing MAEF who was visiting from Fayid. We had a happy and jovial evening during which we had to guess the name of a variety of liqueurs whilst blindfolded. Our two-and-a-half-hour flight to Habbaniya was the shortest of our trips. Here we met briefly Air Vice Marshal Beamish whom Doc had known when living in Northern Ireland before the war, after which we returned to the Transit Mess for the night. Next morning, with the temperature around 50°F, the manicured lawns coated with dew looked superb as they sparkled in the sunlight.

The flight from 'Hab' to Mauripur (Karachi) took seven hours and it was here that things started to go wrong. Indian officials had recently taken over administration of the airfield and, on examining our yellow fever certificates which had been provided by RAF Hospital Wroughton, they declared that a stamp on those of both our flight engineer and radio operator were in the wrong place and they must go into quarantine. We were also told we must get Lyneham to send confirmation that the aircraft had been deloused before leaving.

Ian and John were therefore whisked away to the quarantine quarters whilst the remaining three of us retired to the small RAF Mess. I don't know what the male quarters were like, but I was further depressed to find dirty sheets, a cracked washbasin and a tin hipbath. Our RAF allowance at Karachi with free messing was 5/- a day, the exact price of a bottle of beer, which did nothing to boost our morale. Next day Doc was called to see the Indian authorities and arrived back to tell us that our two crew members must remain in quarantine for ten days. It was now Saturday evening and nothing further could be done. An RAF York which had arrived at Karachi at much the same time as we did was going on next day to Negombo, Ceylon – now Katunayaka, Sri Lanka. Not wishing to stay any longer in Karachi, Doc decided that the three of us would go on too. Without flight engineer or radio officer we therefore set off on the nine hour flight following the York. At RAF Negombo I was allocated a bed in the Nursing Sister's quarters which I thought at the time must be the hardest bed in the Far East, but the bath provided was more than welcome. After dinner in the Mess we sat on the veranda serenaded by frogs and iguanas.

Next day, which was our seventh day out, we rested and had an early night in preparation for the 17,000-mile flight to Singapore. For this the RAF loaned us a radio operator, but we were still without a navigator so I got out the charts, plotted radio bearings, measured drift and tried my hand at keeping some check on our position during the long over water flight. It was some six hours before islands off Sumatra came into sight. The weather, which had been kind to us so far, broke as we approached Singapore where we landed at Changi in a tropical rainstorm. We were delighted to be met by Air Vice Marshal Patch who until recently had been Station Commander at Boscombe Down and was now AOC South-East Asia. He and his wife Tubby took us to their house for a drink before dropping us back at Changi where I had been allocated a double room in the VIP quarters. Next morning the three of us plus a radio operator we had again been loaned were called at 02.30 for a 6 o'clock take-off so that we could reach Darwin in daylight. En route we refuelled at Jakarta which, even in 1951, was suffering civil unrest. The Air Attaché came out to meet us and, whilst Doc went off with him to complete formalities, we remained parked some distance from the airport buildings; we had been advised to remain in the aircraft and watched natives going about their business in tropical rain, carrying either large umbrellas or huge rhubarb-like leaves.

Later, as we flew south down the coast, stormy weather remained with us but over the Timor Sea the clouds thinned. We saw the coast of Australia from quite a distance and had no problem locating Darwin airfield. Here we had barely switched off the engines when an RAAF de-lousing team arrived and before we were allowed to disembark, proceeded to spray the aircraft – too late for me, already plagued with sandfly bites I had collected in Ceylon. When at last we were allowed to get out, a doctor approached with thermometers, which he unceremoniously stuck in our mouths. There was, he told us, a flu epidemic in England, but luckily we were all passed as fit.

Darwin, bombed by the Japanese in the war, was still a remote area. A nursing sister was the only female on the camp and had her own hut which was supported on posts guarded by ant traps; this was where I stayed. After washing and changing I went over to the RAAF Mess where I was the first to be asked what I would like to drink. Wondering what on earth they could best spare in this outpost served only by an occasional boat, I came down on a beer, and immediately regretted it when someone went to a locked fridge and took out a single bottle. The rest of the evening was similarly strained.

We breakfasted next morning at 07.30 and two hours later were airborne for Woomera. We were barely out of the Darwin circuit when revs and boost on No. 1 engine started surging. We had already discovered that there were no maintenance facilities at Darwin and, dreading the thought of imposing ourselves on the RAAF there for what might be several days, we convinced ourselves that it would be better to continue on three engines to somewhere more accessible to maintenance and spares. We followed for the most part the road through Katherine, Daly Waters and Tennants Creek, and were approaching Alice Springs when high oil temperature accompanied by a drop in oil pressure left us no option but to land. I remember looking at the map and remarking that at least there was a railway from 'the Alice' to Adelaide, only to be told later by an Australian that trains ran once a week and that the journey to Adelaide took three days.

At the airfield the 1,900 foot elevation of the 1,100-yard runway left little margin for the two-engined landing and we landed with little to spare. The temperature on the ground was, we found, 100°F, the reason no doubt for our engine problems. We taxied up to the small terminal and disembarked. There we were met by Mr Chamberlain, the local Director of Civil Aviation, who helped us make the necessary phone calls to Woomera. Our next job was to find somewhere to sleep. We found in the town some less than luxurious rooms in the Stuart Arms. Here in these days before air-conditioning, the temperature at 10 pm was still 92°F, hotter than anything I had experienced in Khartoum in the hottest part of the year. Mosquitoes also added to the discomfort, so none of us got much sleep.

Alice Springs, with a population of only some 2,000, was still a small town. It had originally been called Stuart, we were told, after a man who discovered it in 1860. Doc, whose surname was Stuart, proudly announced that this was one of his forebears, eliciting the response: "You would have thought he would have found something better to do."

Next morning we caught a bus back to the airfield, arriving just in time to see an RAAF Lincoln from Woomera landing. While ground crew worked on our Lincoln we stayed in the terminal as it was cooler there than standing in the slight breeze outside. In the terminal Doc, who was wearing a pair of ex Navy shorts, sank into a canvas chair, and this was followed by a ripping sound which we took to be the chair seat giving way; it was in fact his shorts which had split from crutch to waist-band. He therefore got up and backed out of the room clutching the two sides of the split and cursing Miss Pole, the lady who had refused our tropical clothing allowance. At this Squadron Leader Brazier, a dour

Our Lincoln behind the RAAF Lincoln at Alice Springs.

Australian and pilot of the Woomera Lincoln, who was also sitting in the terminal looked up and said: "Now I've seen everything."

We returned to town for a further night, staying this time in the half-built Alice Springs hotel. As before the heat made sleeping virtually impossible and at 3 am I got up and had a shower. On our third day, leaving our aircraft for an engine change, we went on to Woomera with the RAAF, a flight that took two and a half hours. Here, after a late lunch, we were shown to our rooms in the hostel block. When asked whether there was anything I needed, since we had been en route for thirteen days, I said I could do with some washing facilities, whereupon I was shown a washroom complete with ironing board where I could do it myself. Everyone here, I was told, did their own washing and uniforms were only ironed before inspections. I was also shown a broom cupboard containing the necessary tools for cleaning my room. I rested before going back to the Mess for dinner. Everyone went out of their way to make us feel at home but conversation was not easy. Neither did I appreciate the steak which was served for breakfast next morning.

Strict security at Woomera was maintained by siteing buildings as far from each other as possible. A station Dakota flew us next day the three hundred miles to Adelaide, from whence we continued to Melbourne in a TAA Convair. Here our flight engineer Pinkard left us to do his own thing whilst Doc and I continued in a Skymaster to Sydney. I spent a couple of nights with one-time school friend Nancy Fairfax who, amongst other things, took us to Bondi Beach to swim; I still have memories of the strings of stinging jellyfish washed up on the beach there.

We left Australia in a BOAC Constellation which refuelled at Darwin; here we disembarked for a wash, refuelling again at Jakarta en route to Singapore. Here we again stayed in the Changi Mess and had two happy days, collected again by Sam and Tubby Patch and taken to lunch in their house high above Changi village with a glorious view over the Johore Straits. From here we saw a passing ship with the unusual name Flying Enterprise which not long afterwards became headlines in the UK when it was stranded on a reef off Lands End and its Captain refused to be lifted off. After lunch we were taken to 'down town' Singapore to sightsee and shop before we had dinner at Seaview. I particularly remember Sam Patch saying, as we drove down a main street and passed a wide side-turning: "If you went down there you would never be seen again."

Our journey home was in a Qantas Constellation with refuelling stops at Calcutta and Karachi and a night stop at Cairo, where we inevitably 'did' the Pyramids. We made London next day after a further refuelling stop at Rome. We had left the UK on 19th February and arrived back on 18th March. Our two crew members whom we left in Karachi spent ten boring days of confinement, during which alcoholic refreshment was strictly limited. They made their trip to Australia later in a Boscombe Hastings.

CHAPTER 24

FAIREY'S

By 1953 the amount of work coming into the Civil Aircraft Test Section at A&AEE Boscombe was significantly reduced as civil aircraft manufacturers took over clearance tests on their own aircraft. I had also been advised by Mr Hufton, Superintendent of Performance at the A&AEE, that as I had come into the Civil Service 'by the back door,' I was unlikely to be offered promotion. I had had virtually no flying since the Viscount tropical trials in August 1952, and my only work was writing up reports, so I started looking round for an alternative job. I remember applying for one with a French aviation company – which I was strongly advised not to take, even if offered it – and with Shell, but I eventually settled for one in the Flight Development Department of Fairey Aviation at White Waltham where they were completing final clearance tests on the Fairey Gannet.

Before being taken on I was interviewed by their Chief Engineer, Robert (later Sir Robert) Lickley, who before joining Fairey's had been Professor of Aircraft Design at Cranfield. At the interview he asked me amongst other things what I wanted to be paid and, not being commercially minded, I almost certainly quoted what I was being paid at Boscombe. As a civil servant in days before there were commitments to equal pay, I was probably paid less there than men doing the same job; anyway he suggested I asked more!

I left Boscombe at the end of February 1953 with quite a few regrets as I had had a happy time there, but I felt it was time to move on. At White Waltham, Group Captain Gordon Slade was chief test pilot and Peter Twiss DSO & Bar, a wartime Fleet Air Arm pilot, his second. The Chief Flight Development engineer was Maurice Child, head of the section I was about to join. Whilst at Boscombe I had acquired a Wicko, a small two-seater aircraft in which I had taken part in a number of air races. Before I arrived at White Waltham, Gordon had told me that I would not be allowed to keep the Wicko in the Fairey hangar; I had therefore decided that it would have to be sold.

I had recently traded in my Lancia Augusta CUW66, which I bought in 1939, for a small Ford van which would be of more use when I was on the move. Thus it was that on 1st March 1953 I packed my possessions into the van and drove, first to Thruxton to try and interest the Wiltshire Flying Club in buying the Wicko, and from there on to Paley Street, a village near White Waltham, where Philip Wills the renowned glider pilot and his wife had offered to put me up whilst I looked for somewhere permanent to live. This in a couple of weeks turned out to be a flat in another nearby village, Waltham St. Lawrence. The Fairey design office and factory was at Hayes and as their own grass airfield, the original Heathrow, had been swallowed up by the new Heathrow Airport, they had been given a lease on the grass airfield at White Waltham which in 1942 had been bought by the Ministry of Aircraft Production and was still in government hands.

When I joined Fairey's in 1953 the Gannet, which had suffered a number of delays in its clearance for the Royal Navy, was still a year or so away from squadron service. Completion of the trials called for before it could be handed over was a top priority. Amongst the outstanding trials awaiting completion were hot-weather trials. As I had taken part in a number of these whilst at Boscombe, this I assume, was one of the reasons I was being taken on. When I joined Fairey's, tests were being carried out on the second AS.1 Gannet prototype VR557, an anti-submarine and strike aircraft fitted with the newly developed Double Mamba engine. This was made up of two coupled Mamba propeller-turbine engines operating through a common gear box, driving two contra-rotating propellers. A major advantage of this design was that in cruising flight when full power was not needed, one engine could be shut down and the propeller feathered, extending the aircraft's range and also reducing maintenance. Another advantage as far as the Royal Navy was concerned was that as the Double Mamba ran on kerosene, therefore carriers would not have to store petrol for it.

By the time I joined Fairey's, Gannets had been on test with both Fairey and Fleet Air Arm pilots for a number of months. As a new member of the firm, my job was simply to record in-flight measurements, analyse them and produce a report on the results. There were still a number of flight tests to be completed before the aircraft could be

Fairey Gannet

handed over to the Fleet Air Arm. My first flights were in the back seat of Gannet VR557, measuring fuel consumption in level flight at various heights as there was concentration at the time on meeting the Ministry's range requirements.

Our Chief Engineer, after a disagreement with Boscombe Down over some Gannet tests carried out there, had got clearance for the firm to carry out all further Gannet tests itself in conjunction with the Royal Navy. As part of this a month later, VR557 was taken by Fairey's to the Royal Navy station at Halfar in Malta for performance measurements at air temperatures higher than those available in England. The aircraft was flown to Malta by Lieutenant Commander Hallett. The Fairey team, which included test pilot Peter Twiss and myself, flew to Malta in a British European Airways Viking. At Halfar I was put up by the WRENs in their house in Kalifrana. The Naval officers at Halfar were not particularly welcoming to females or even to their own WRENs, and although the WRENs' house was too far away to go back to for lunch, I was not allowed to join our crew in the wardroom. Amongst the naval ground crew however there was a Petty Officer who insisted on giving me his daily quota of rum! After some ten days during which we obtained the required performance measurements we returned to England, again by BEA.

In the late summer flight tests started at White Waltham on the first production Gannet, WN339, tests which continued until the following summer. In November 1954 a team made up of Lieutenant

Des Cassidi with Gannet in Khartoum, November 1954. ELC in the back.

Commander, later Admiral, Desmond Cassidi from the Fleet Air Arm Intensive Trials Flight, Roy Morris, test pilot for Fairey's and Peter Aked from Armstrong Siddeley's, took WN372 to Khartoum for tropical trials where I joined them as test observer. At Khartoum we were attached to A&AEE's Tropical Testing Unit, which I knew well from my days at Boscombe Down. The unit still held bicycles for use by trials crews to get around on including a lady's one for me! It was whilst there on what was sadly my last visit to Khartoum, that an Askari stopped me bicycling down an empty one-way street. This left me feeling that the British presence in the Sudan must be coming to an end – and sadly it was!

On its return from Khartoum, WN372 was fitted with an up rated engine, turning it into the prototype Gannet AS.4 It was with this that in July 1956 I went out to Idris, Tripoli, with Lieutenant Commander Peter Davis to take more performance measurements under tropical conditions. The night before we left in a Hastings from Boscombe Down, I had been dining with Dick Fairey who was living in Henley-on-Thames. Arriving home late, I stubbed my toe on a brick while getting out of my car and the next morning was unable to put on my shoe; I could however walk OK in sandals so continued on my way as planned. In Tripoli, with my toe still sore, it was suggested that I visit the Army medical section downtown where a young lad X-rayed it and said simply: "It's broke." As nothing could be done about it I went back to the airfield and carried on with the flight tests as arranged.

We only made four flights from Idris, but completed one of our main tasks, which was to take temperature measurements on the engine when running at 45°C, the temperature officially listed as 'tropical maximum.' We didn't reach this temperature until a Sunday when we had given the ground crew a day off to visit ruins at Sabratha; Peter Davis and I however had stayed in case the temperature rose to the magic 45° and whilst waiting decided to play tennis. As we played the temperature rose higher and higher until the tennis balls hung in the air and the surface of the court burnt my feet through my shoes! So giving up our tennis we checked on the air temperature, to find that 45° was being recorded. Without the help of ground crew, we therefore pushed the aircraft out of the hangar and ran the engine to take the required readings.

ELC climbing aboard e Gannet.

To get home we were collected by a Bristol Freighter from Boscombe Down, night-stopping en route at Dijon where we stayed in the Chapeau Rouge. We made a late start the next morning after being delayed by some of the naval ground crew who had overslept after a heavy night out. With the Airborne Early Warning (AEW) Gannet now well on the way, this was the last of the overseas performance trials carried out by Fairey's on an AS.1. In the redesigned AEW Gannet, the bomb-bay was replaced by a large radome and a larger rear cockpit provided room for two radar operators.

Many of the early Gannet sea trials had been completed on carriers, but I could not take part in them as women were not allowed to spend a night at sea. In August 1957 a very special day visit to Ark Royal was arranged for me by Commander (later Admiral) Douglas Parker who, when I was at Boscombe, had been in 'C' Squadron. I was picked up early in the morning in a helicopter from Ford and, once on board, was allotted the Captain's day cabin. Before being picked up in the evening by the helicopter I had been shown over the whole ship. I have very special memories of our departure when the crew lined up below, saluting as the helicopter climbed vertically over the deck, as they would no doubt have done for a VIP.

I was keeping up my flying by taking the occasional flight in Fairey Flying Club aircraft; these operated in conjunction with the West London Aero Club on the east side of the airfield. The Fairey aircraft included Tipsy 1 two-seater G-AISC, which we called the tin bath, and Auster G-AHAY. I sometime took friends for flights in the Tipsy. I also flew Fairey Junior G-AMVP which was kept in the Fairey hangar and which on one occasion, I stood on its nose and broke the propeller; this wasn't entirely my fault as a ballast weight which should have been in the rear fuselage was missing. My pre-war commercial 'B' licence was also still valid and this enabled me to act as second pilot in the Fairey Air Survey Dakota based at White Waltham when a rule was introduced that they must carry two pilots when on photographic missions. By 1954, with only the odd trip in a Gannet coming up, I found myself called on to do more and more jobs in the Rapides which Fairey's used for general communication.

My first Rapide job came in October 1953 when Dick Fairey asked me to come with him to Cambridge and then take the Rapide back to White Waltham. After this I was asked to do more and more Rapide jobs, somewhat to the displeasure of Maurice Child, my head of section, who had always wanted to be a pilot himself! More often than not it was to return an aircraft used by one of the test pilots to position themselves at another airfield. Also, when Gannet tests arose, such as Dummy Deck Landings (ADDLS)– which had to be carried out on a runway – or catapult tests, I would fly the Gannet ground crew over in the Rapide before taking part in the tests myself in the back cockpit of the Gannet.

de Havilland
Dragon Rapide

I also made trips in the Rapide to Avion Fairey, Fairey's subsidiary company in Belgium at Gosselies near Charleroi. The factory had been founded between the wars by Ernest Tips where, amongst many other things, the two seater side-by-side Tipsy B light aircraft was designed and built. In 1940 the factory was destroyed by German bombs; much of the equipment however was salvaged and shipped to Britain in a destroyer. To get to England factory staff boarded the Cunard liner *Lancastria* which on the way over was dive-bombed and sunk, eight of the Fairey staff being lost. During the war Tips worked in England but after the war returned to Belgium to rebuild the factory which re-opened in October 1946, with contracts to repair and overhaul an assortment of military and civil aircraft. Between 1950 and 1951 the size of the factory was extended and more staff taken on to meet a contract to build Meteor Mk.8 fighters for the Belgian Air Force. My hour-and-a-half flights to Gosselies, which always started at Blackbushe, were no doubt to take parts over to them. I invariably came back with presents of fresh coffee beans, probably from Rhodesia where they had contacts, and which were something still relatively rare in England.

There are a number of Rapide flights that I particularly remember. On one I collected Dick Fairey and his son Charles from Gatwick because Dick, involved in a divorce, was not for some legal reason allowed to fly Charles himself. I also recall being sent to pick up a Flight photographer from Hamble to take photos of the last Firefly.

The longest trip shown in my log book took place in June 1955 when I was sent to Donibristle to collect some IFF aerials, a journey which took over six hours, so I was now having no problem in doing enough flying to keep my licence valid. When tests started on the Fairey Delta 2 the amount of taxi work increased significantly as the FD.2 was based for the most part at Boscombe Down, later carrying out tests from Thurleigh and eventually Bedford. For these a Rapide was often needed in which after the tests, Peter Twiss could fly himself home. Amongst these I have special memories of one occasion when the FD.2 was scheduled to appear at the 1955 SBAC show, but was not allowed into Farnborough until the braking tail parachute was cleared for full operation. Thus it was that on the Saturday before the show opened, last-minute checks to show that the parachute opened correctly were being carried out at Thurleigh, an airfield not yet officially open. The FD.2 was already there and work on the parachute was already in hand. I left from White Waltham with Peter in the Rapide early on Saturday morning so that when the tail parachute was cleared, Peter could take the FD.2 to Farnborough and I could take the Rapide to wherever it was wanted next. Come lunchtime, with work still going OK on the Delta and no facilities as yet on the airfield, some of us walked off the airfield to a nearby pub to get some food.

The Fairey Delta 2

On returning to the airfield, we were challenged by a security guard who said: "Women are not allowed on this airfield." To this Peter replied without stopping: "This one is flying an aircraft," and as we continued on our way, the security guard remained rooted to the spot, trying to work out no doubt what his answer to that should be!

Another trip which I particularly remember was one on a rough and gusty day on which I was called on to take a Rapide to Boscombe so that Peter could fly himself home. At Boscombe the rarely-used short runway was more or less into the strong wind, and managing to get down on it, I found the group awaiting collection standing by the runway so as to avoid any necessity for taxiing. Much relieved at the arrival of the Rapide without stopping the engines, Peter climbed in, went up front and flew us back to White Waltham.

In July 1955 Bruce Campbell, a long-time friend of mine and one-time de Havilland test pilot, as well as owning a boat in the south of France, had a de Havilland two-seater Hornet Moth registered G-ADNE. From his boat, then in the south of France, he asked me to fly the Hornet down to Cannes for both of us to fly home in.

I had been living in Berkshire since 1952 and playing in inter-club tennis matches for my club at Peppard for a number of years and had been awarded my Berkshire County Tennis Colours. So in July 1955 I was at Hunstanton playing for Berkshire in the annual inter-counties tennis week in which groups of six counties play one another. In each group the county winning the most matches was promoted to a higher group, whilst the one winning the least went down to the group below. In both the mens' and ladies' groups, No.1 Group contains the best counties.

Friday 22 July was the last day of our matches at Hunstanton. I rushed to my car as soon as I had finished playing our last match against Dorset, and set out for Panshanger, a grass airfield in Hertfordshire, to collect Bruce's Hornet. By the time I got there it was already eight o'clock and as I had in any case to land at Southend to clear Customs, I decided to spend the night there. Next morning I left Southend, landing at Le Touquet to clear Customs. I next refuelled at Nevers and after that at Marseille where, as it was already seven o'clock and I didn't know how to contact Bruce, I spent another night. The next morning I continued to Cannes where I was met by Bruce, the overall journey from Panshanger to Cannes having taken eight and a half hours.

We had three happy days on the boat, including a trip to St. Tropez, from which the return trip holds special memories. Bruce had hired a man to look after the boat when he was in England and he was steering at a time when Bruce decided he was going too near the rocks. When asking him to move further off the coast brought about no change of course, Bruce in an aside to me said: "If I take over I shall have to sack him" which, as he was about to leave for England would have been highly inconvenient. We got back to Cannes without Bruce taking over! The following evening Bruce, in his indifferent French, rang ordering a taxi for early next morning but was unsure as to whether his French had been understood. Next morning the taxi nevertheless arrived to take us to the airfield and shortly before six thirty we were airborne for our first stop at Lyons. Bruce, who had a bad back, worried me a lot by every now and then putting his full weight on the frame above the cockpit to relieve pain in his back, but luckily no damage resulted. After refuelling at Lyons we cleared customs at Toussot-le-Noble before crossing the Channel to Southend.

Bruce was living at the time in Herringfleet Hall near Yarmouth which had its own landing strip; this was covered with rapidly sprouting bracken which therefore rendered it unusable for landing after a very short time. We landed and were picked up by car from nearby North Denes. We had set off from Cannes at around at 7.30 am and landed at North Denes a little after 8.30 pm on a clear summer evening; the flight home had taken us just under eleven hours, a one day record for the Hornet, we felt!

But there is more to this story. A week or two later Bruce took the Hornet to Hamble to collect his boat Rinancy, and in due course I took it back for him to North Denes. Michael Dible, to whom I had sold my Wicko, had come up to collect me. We spent the night in Rinancy, now moored off Great Yarmouth, and next morning set off in the Wicko for White Waltham. In rain and low cloud we were forced to make an emergency landing at Stradishall, then an American Air Force base, where we were not well received! After some argument we were allowed to leave the Wicko there and were picked up by Michael's brother John who came up by car to collect us. Next day I hired the Fairey Flying Club Tipsy and flew Michael back to Stradishall to collect the Wicko. At the time of writing, rising fifty years later, G-ADNE is still serviceable and in private ownership.

During my time with Fairey's I had a once-in-a-lifetime holiday in the Bahamas. Bahama Airlines was run by BOAC, and in charge of it was BOAC Captain Peter Fair whose wife, Winnie Crossley, had been one of the first eight women pilots to join ATA. She was at Hatfield when I joined and was someone I came to know well.

*innie and
ter Fair

Eddy Ballard, an American ATA pilot, had returned to his business in North America when he left ATA. He soon sold up and moved to the warmer climate of Nassau, where he took a job as a pilot for Bahama Airlines. He and his wife Ruth, who had been one of my contemporaries at Hatfield, were now living in Nassau and in 1957, they invited me to stay with them for Christmas.

Thus on 21st December 1957 I arrived at Heathrow at around 8.30 pm, where I was joined by a bunch of Fairey test pilots who had called in for a meal. It was not till 12.40 am that I was called to board the Pan American DC-7 for New York. Because of a 50 mph headwind, we were then told we would be landing to refuel at Shannon, so it was not until about 3.30 am that we finally took off from there and settled down shortly afterwards to a much needed meal.

At New York Ann Wood, another ex-ATA American pilot, had arranged for me to stay in Jaqueline Cochran's apartment in 52nd Street, where I particularly recall a large compass rose set into the hall floor. I spent two nights in New York doing the rounds, which included going to the top of the Empire State Building where I acquired a badge, which I still have, on which is written: "I've been on top."

Two days before Christmas I arrived at Windsor Field, Nassau, again in a DC-7C, full of young Americans going to the Bahamas for

Christmas. Here I was met by both Winnie and Ruth. Ruth's mother had now joined them in Nassau and lived in a house adjacent to their own. This then was where I was to sleep, and it was here that I was first introduced to tea-bags – which in those days I recall thinking was not quite 'the thing'!

The weather when I arrived consisted of pouring rain and gales. Peter Fair had arranged that during my visit I could fly as second pilot in any Bahamas Air Lines aircraft but to make things legal, I must be issued with a ticket for each flight showing 100% rebate. My first trip when the weather improved was on 29th December with Ed Ballard in a Grumman Goose amphibian. We went to Mangrove Cay, Andros and, while there were neither passengers or freight for the trip there, as Eddy remarked, there were two 'egg-heads' to be brought back to Nassau. But at Andros no passengers appeared. Instead a black man in his Sunday best rowed out to meet us in a dinghy, shouting to Ed who was up front letting out the anchor that there were no passengers waiting and that he was on his way to church! On our return to Nassau Ed's next scheduled job was in a Herald to George Town, but the Herald turned out to be unserviceable and he was given the rest of the day off. Five days later I had a flight in the Catalina to Harbour Island with Captain Welch. After that I had another flight, again in the Catalina, stopping at five places

Pilot House Club, Nassau, Bahamas 28/12/57. L-R; Ann Wood-Kelly, ELC, Ruth Ballard, Winnie Fair (wife of Peter Fair then head of BOAC Bahamas)

which my log book shows as Sandy Point, Hope Town, Marsh Harbour, Man-of-War Cay and Green Turtle Cay. Back at Nassau the Catalina was beached as always to avoid taking in water.

About the most memorable trip I had out there was in the Grumman Goose with Bill Quick. We had set out for Harbour Island where Alan Butler, Chairman of de Havillands, had a house which from time to time Winnie went over to check. We were nearing the Island when Bill, who had been pointing out landmarks on distant Eleuthera, saw puffs of smoke coming from the port engine. As the fuel gauge showed adequate fuel he opened the cross-feed to allow fuel to be fed to the port engine from the starboard tank. This brought no response so, increasing power on the starboard engine, Bill shouted through the door to his passengers that there was a spot of bother. But by opening up the starboard engine and raising the nose he managed to maintain height and we carried on.

At Harbour Island a dinghy was sent out to take Winnie and her maid off whilst I was left sitting in the second pilot's seat, to help Bill beach the aircraft, contributing to the manoeuvre in any way I could. In due course we got the Goose up on the slipway, where it had to remain until engineers came from Nassau to repair the engine. Once the aircraft was safely ashore Bill and I disembarked and joined Winnie. By now she had walked up to the house and we found her walking round the garden with the gardener, who had just been asked to cut down a large bunch of bananas for her to take back to Nassau. In the evening we walked downtown to a small restaurant where a pianist, who during the summer worked in Majorca, played to us while we ate.

When we got back to the house after dinner, Bill and I walked in the dark round the island, famous for its pink sands. Somehow we all found somewhere to sleep in the empty house. When I woke in the morning I decided that a cup of tea would go down well; but there was no tea, and all I could find were tins of beer, so I took those round instead!

The following day we were collected by a Widgeon belonging to the Mayor of New York, which was at Nassau for the winter.

I had two more flights with Bahama Airlines in the Heron with Eddie Ballard, and on January 10th flew to Miami in a British West Indies Viscount. This was followed by a flight in a National Airlines DC-7C to

Washington. Here I stayed with friends over three nights and was taken to see the Smithsonian and many other prominent memorials. The weather was bright but very cold and there were few other people around. At one stage I climbed to the top of one of the taller Memorials and, on reaching the top, found somebody already there who greeted me by name. He was English and I recognised the face but couldn't for the life of me place him. I asked questions that I hoped would give me a clue as to who he was, and even thought of going to look at the register in the hotel in which he was staying. Sometime later the name came to me; it was Peter Clifford, a competitor I had met at various UK air races, and therefore had no specific place to which I could relate him. After Washington I flew up to Boston with Northeast Airlines for a short stay with Ann Wood, who lived in nearby Manchester. Whilst there I visited Boston and also Gloucester! I returned home on 18th January in a BOAC DC-7C, landing for breakfast at Prestwick and then, for some reason, landing once more at Burtonwood before reaching London Airport, from where I took a taxi home: the end of a very special holiday.

CHAPTER 25

POST-FAIREY'S

In February 1960 Westland Aircraft put in an offer for Fairey Aviation consisting, so the papers said, of £1,400,000 cash and two million five shilling shares for the entire share capital of Fairey Aviation. Before effecting the merger Duncan Sands, Minister of Aviation, was consulted and was reported in the papers as having welcomed the arrangement. Westland had already taken over Bristol's and Saunders Roe helicopters and again according to the papers, had undertaken to carry on with the Rotodyne project. As a result of the takeover Robert Lickley resigned at the end of March from all his appointments in Fairey's. In June, Dick Fairey retired from the Board of Directors and relinquished his position as Vice-Chairman of the Fairey Company Ltd which he had held since 1956. Dr George Hislop, formerly Fairey's chief Designer (Helicopters), who had been responsible for development of the Rotodyne, joined Westland's as Chief Engineer (Aircraft) and became head of, amongst other things, Fairey Flight Development.

In my last days with Fairey's, with all work at White Waltham other than that on the Rotodyne coming to an end, I was sent to Hayes to work in the wind tunnel – which was not at all my scene – and where I was not allowed to use the senior Mess. I was given by Dr Hislop the choice of going to Yeovil but, as Westlands were not interested in fixed wing aircraft and it was not clear what I would do if I went there, I did not accept. I was also worried about how they would accept a woman there. Lickley, on retiring from Fairey's, had joined Hawkers and had suggested to me that there could be a job for me with Hawkers at Dunsfold. In 1961, although the development of the vertical take-off P.1154 was well under way, the new Labour Government under Harold Wilson decided that there were enough technical developments under way for the Navy and the Air Force. The money could be better spent they decided, by buying American Phantoms and scrapping plans for further development of both the TSR.2 and the P.1154.

Jobs at Hawkers were being lost rather than new ones taken on; I therefore took a job I had been offered in the flight development department of Folland, who were working at Dunsfold on clearance of the Folland Gnat, which was having problems fulfilling its supersonic role. I had recently bought a house in Twyford, Berkshire and decided to see how things went before selling it and moving to Surrey. For the first few weeks, I drove down to Dunsfold, a distance of over fifty miles, each day. After a week or two I found somewhere in Cranleigh where from Monday to Friday I was given bed and breakfast. It was just as well that I did not move house as from the start I did not get on with the head of the Folland flight development department who, unlike Lickley, tended to refer decisions back to Boscombe Down. He was probably in a difficult position since Petter was no longer around to advise.

At lunchtime, sitting with other Hawker employees, we continually discussed what contracts, if any, could be expected to come in but as winter drew on and nothing was forthcoming, I decided that Dunsfold was not for me and applied for a job with the Ministry of Civil Aviation. Surely, I thought, my practical experience since working for the Ministry in 1948 would be of some use to them. Although they took me back this wasn't the way it worked out.

In February 1962 I started work at Heathrow with the newly-formed Air Traffic Control Experimental Unit (ATCEU). This had been started up under Don Lipman to develop the first printed flight progress strips. At this time Air Traffic Controllers were still working from raw radar displays and I recall that around this time, the first digital radar signals came in from Burrington. I also recall being sent on what was called an ATC Computer course at Brunel College, where we were introduced to flow charts and design of electrical circuits, also on a statistics course. I was still at the ATCEU when Lipman left to join Eurocontrol. Shortly afterwards the ATCEU under John Goodyear was moved to Bournemouth, Hurn and I was posted to London. In London I started work in Woburn Place where my Director was ex BOAC Captain Vernon Hunt, and my head of branch Group Captain E. A. Johnston whose father, the navigator on the R.101 airship, had been killed when it crashed at Beauvais in October 1930 en route to India.

In 1962, after a life of flying in the RAF, Group Captain Johnston had been posted to a ground job in the National Air Traffic Control Service (NATCS), which he wasn't very happy about. The Directorate I had joined had the job of producing paperwork essential before government money could be allocated for building what is now, in very much enlarged form, a joint Military and Civil Air Traffic Control Centre at West Drayton. In order to speed production of these plans, a special Linesman Mediator Project team was set up under Air Commodore Hunter Todd. Because they said that I was making a useful contribution to report-writing in Hunt's Directorate – I was after all, more accustomed to report writing than most of the ex-RAF people there – I found myself included in the team when DPLM was formed and this was the only time I can say that I enjoyed working for the Civil Service.

The DPLM team consisted of selected Military and Civil Air Traffic Controllers, ranked from Squadron Leader to Wing Commander, the head of our section being Group Captain Roy Manger. The senior civil telecommunications engineer was D.G. Terrington and amongst the junior tels staff I particularly remember Harry Powell, brother of Robert Powell the film actor. Wing Commander Vick, who represented the Defence Staff, I also have special reasons to remember.

As our work was highly classified, junior staff had to take it in turn to leave last in the evening after checking that no cabinets had been left open or paperwork left on desks or even in a waste paper basket. One night when I was 'duty dog' the only unlocked cabinet was the most 'secret' one of all, that of Wing Commander Vick. He had closed his padlock but without putting it through the necessary loops, so without the key it could not be relocked. Sorting this out resulted in an unusually late night for me! If the security staff came round after we had all gone home found and cabinets open or classified paperwork out, next morning we would find all cabinets pasted up with sticky tape! At one stage I shared an office with a Squadron Leader who continually smoked a pipe, something which in those days one couldn't complain about. When I suggested that if he did this at home his house must need a great deal of cleaning, he told me that he didn't smoke at home and that when he came up in the train from Kent, he sat in a non-smoking carriage!

Later all the 'juniors' were moved into one large office where I got to know ex-RAF engineer Cyril Thatcher, who had on his desk a three-inch solid metal ball which he told us, had been a ball-bearing on a radar head which he had serviced during the war. This can't have done him any good as he died not long after. Cyril, an avid stamp collector, encouraged me to look again at my very modest stamp collection. At the time there were as well as Stanley Gibbons a number of stamp dealers and stamp arcades in the Strand. These we would visit at lunchtime. From my purchases I built up my collection which in later years I exhibited at STAMPEX, the international stamp show.

DPLM was based in the Adelphi, but at one stage was transferred to Mintech and we moved to First Avenue House in New Oxford Street. During this period I attended meetings at Malvern with Marconi, one of the main contractors for the work at West Drayton. I would go up by train the night before and, after booking in at an hotel, would walk, weather permitting, on the Malvern hills. Somehow the plans we put together for West Drayton must have been approved as in a much advanced state, the Air Traffic Control Centre is still there today.

In September 1962 I was lucky enough to be asked to crew in a boat entered for the Cowes to Torquay Daily Express powerboat race. I had already taken part in a number of air races but the offshore powerboat race was something special. My long-time friend Bruce Campbell had a boatyard at Hamble where he built 'Christina' powerboats. He had entered five of them for the 1962 race, one of which he proposed to race himself; another he had entered for his wife Pamela and this was the boat I had been asked to crew. We would be the only all-woman crew and as our boat Thunderbolt I, with its 650 bhp engine, had won the race the previous year when driven by Tommy Sopwith so it was one of the favourites.

I was working at Dunsfold at that time and on the Friday night before the race I went down to Hamble to stay the night with the Campbells. At the yard that night all was hassle with people chasing missing parts, tuning their engines and generally checking whether their boats would be ready for the start next day. A number of well-known names from the flying world were entered for the race, some of whom we knew well: Peter Twiss, who with the closure of Fairey Aviation

TLC and Pamela Campbell in the Cowes-Torquay Powerboat Race.

was now working for Fairey Marine, had been entered by C.G. James in his Fairey Huntress, and Charles Currey had been entered by Major Chichester-Smith in his Fairey Huntsman. Jeffrey Quill was driving for R.S. Wilkins in Vosper's Tramontana which had twin engines giving a total of 2,308 bhp. But Tommy Sopwith, down to race in Thunderbolt II, another of Bruce's boats and a potential record-breaker, sadly missed the start.

The start, which took place at 10 am, was governed by flags from the Royal Yacht Squadron; the pace was set at some forty knots by the Royal Navy's Brave Borderer. I have a photograph of the start but am unable to pick out our boat. The length of the Cowes to Torquay course was shown as 170 miles and as in air races, it was a case of maintaining full throttle all the way, whatever the sea conditions. From Cowes the route, marked for the most part by buoys, was round the Nab Tower, back to the Needles and thereafter along the south coast to Portland Bill. After that there was some fifty miles of open sea to the Skerries Buoy off the Devon coast south of Berry Head. Here the sea was rough and we were constantly thrown into the air, only to crash back immediately onto the water. At one stage, after a particularly large wave hit us while I was standing next to Pamela, my knees bent to such an extent that my seat actually hit the bottom of ·the boat before I bounced up again! We arrived at Skerries in 6th place but, on the way back to Teignmouth and the finish at Torquay, fuel-feed trouble intervened when we were rounding the Thatcher Rock with only a mile or so to go. Without an engine we were unable to complete the course. Very disappointing for both for us, the only all-woman crew and in the running for a prize, but even more so for Bruce, whose own boat, as well as Tommy Sopwith's, had been non-starters. At Torquay rooms had been booked for us, but the room booked for me was for some reason claimed by Dr Savundra and I had to move out. In the evening there was prize-giving and a dance, during which I heard one of a couple circling near us saying: "I was sitting on my adjustable seat" a luxury for those days – "when it collapsed".

The winner of the race was Jeffrey Quill in Tramontana at an average speed of 32 kt, during which it was said that his two engines burnt 525 gallons of petrol. Sad that we didn't finish the race, but for me anyway it was certainly an experience.

Coming back in after our fuel failure.

CHAPTER 26

'FORGOTTEN PILOTS'

When DPLM ended I had the job of planning a method of use of the new Secondary Surveillance Radar (SSR). This was an extension into civil use of the Identification Friend or Foe system (IFF) used by military aircraft. Up to this time it had not been compulsory for civil aircraft to be fitted with transponders, the equipment enabling them to be identified and tracked by Air Traffic Control on their radar screens. In connection with this work, I went to Brussels from time to time for Eurocontrol conferences.

It was also around this period that I started research into my history of the Air Transport Auxiliary. Before the end of the war BOAC had sponsored Brief Glory, a Harborough publication published in 1946. The man chosen to write this was E.C. Cheesman, a statistics officer at ATA Headquarters White Waltham. This gives useful details of how the various Ferry Pools were set up, together with stories from a selected number of early pilots. Written for the most part before the close-down of ATA, official records of its flying would not yet have been available. I felt the ATA was all about flying and that this was the side that needed to be recorded. Twenty years after the end of the war the Public Record Office was still in Chancery Lane, London. As I was working in the Adelphi this was somewhere that I could get to by bus so, forgetting about stamps, I now spent my lunchtimes going through documents held there that referred to the work of ATA. Anything I thought was of interest I recorded on my tape-recorder, went home and spent the evening typing out on my old-fashioned typewriter.

Another of my sources of information was the Beaverbrook library where the librarian, A.J.P. Taylor, allowed me to go through Lord Beaverbrook's cabinets which had not yet been opened. Sadly, however, there was little in them that referred to his time in charge of ATA. However, in History of the Second World War, an HMSO book, British war production figures showed the number of each type of aircraft that had been built. Added to this the PRO had records divided into types of all the aircraft ferried by ATA.

In due course the time came for me to start looking for a publisher. Turned down by the well known ones I at last came across Foulis, a publisher owned by John Hassell who ran his own business until being taken over by Haynes. Living in Henley only a few miles from my house, communication with him was exceptionally easy; I can't remember when we started work but he would come over and pick up my roughly typed pages and get them properly typed and edited. I remember him telling me, when the book eventually came out, that five hand-typed drafts had been made – for these were days before the general availability of computers. He published a hard-back edition in 1971 at £4.50 which was well reviewed – except by the ATA Association, who refused even to mention it in their newsletters. I was working in the Flight Operations Inspectorate (FOI) when it was published and when I told my head of section that a book I had written had been published, he simply said that he was not interested in novels! But as a documentary, in a small way it soon took on.

A year or two later Mr Hassell's business was taken over by Haynes. When the first edition sold out I wrote to Haynes asking about a second edition. By now Haynes were only interested in motor books so instead, they gave me back my copyright. Thus in 1982 I found a printer in Reading who undertook to print 1,000 soft-back copies which I set about selling myself. It did not take long for me however to find out that I was no salesman. Bookshops, it seemed, expected you to call round every few weeks with stocks for which you were not immediately paid. However, people soon started writing in to me for copies even from America; these I packaged up and posted until all the copies I held were sold. I even sold copies which had been rejected by the printer but had no obvious faults. I have one such copy acquired by Air Marshal Sir Arthur Harris, which he signed and returned to me. Eventually In 1985 Robin Read's company, Nelson and Saunders Ltd, undertook a further hard-back edition but unfortunately his company was forced into liquidation and it was not until 1998 that a further soft-back edition of Forgotten Pilots was taken on by CAA publisher Westward Digital Ltd, now Documedia, who at the time of writing still supply it.

In 1937 when the 11th Duchess of Bedford – better known as "the Flying Duchess" was lost at sea on her last flight, Richard Riding, then editor of Aeroplane Monthly suggested that I write an article for his magazine about her. This I did and, when researching the subject, got so interested in it that I went on to turn it into a book, which was published by Air Research in 1993.

When DPLM closed I was posted to the Flight Operations Inspectorate, a branch of the newly formed Civil Aviation Authority which was responsible for overseeing civil aircraft operators, and here I remained for the next six years; but I was never really happy there. When I joined the FOI, it was at this time based in The Adelphi; I have few memories of this large and dreary building, but one of them is of when, at a time of bomb scares, one of our junior staff left a cardboard box outside the lift. This was considered to be a possible bomb and resulted in us all having to leave the building. We heard afterwards that the man who put the box by the lift was given instant dismissal – a rare occurrence I imagine in the civil service!

In 1975 an American ATA friend Ed Heering, invited me to come and stay at his home in Hayward, California. He was at the time, Chief Pilot of World Airways which was owned by Ed Daly, and had persuaded Daly to give me a non revenue pass from Gatwick to Oakland.

*LC with
d Heering,
os Angeles
975.*

Having always heard of California as a land of sunshine, in a cold, damp and cheerless English January the invitation strongly appealed so I contacted Mike Deasy, World Airways representative in the UK, to ask what flights there were available from Gatwick to Oakland. There were a number of flights out he told me, but few coming back so we decided to wait and see whether things improved around Easter. Eventually I settled for a flight that left on Easter Saturday and duly 'booked out' from my office in London for two weeks.

I spent Good Friday cleaning the house and eating any remnants of food in the fridge and on Saturday morning I was packed and ready to go, when the phone rang to tell me that the flight would be coming to Gatwick fully booked and there would be no room for me. The Sunday flight I was told had been cancelled, and would I please up ring them on Monday. It snowed here over Easter leaving me with no plans and it was beginning to look as if I would have no plans for the coming fortnight! However, I rang on Monday and was told that a flight was expected on Tuesday which would be leaving at 15.00 hours. On Tuesday at about midday I was again ready to leave the house, when the phone rang to tell me that the aircraft had become unserviceable, it was still coming but they said they didn't know when! I therefore rang back at two-hourly intervals for news and each time was told that the flight was still coming, but they still didn't know when. By 8.30pm, not wishing to miss it, I therefore took the train to West Drayton from whence there was a bus to Gatwick, due to arrive there at around 11pm. At Gatwick I spent the rest of the night between the World Airways office and the all night restaurant. The plane eventually arrived and was due to leave at 07.45 next morning, by which time I had already been up for 24 hours!

The aircraft, a 'stretched' DC8, was uncomfortably full, but nothing mattered now as I was at last on my way. At JFK we were turned out to clear customs after which we pushed our bags on trollies to the domestic terminal. Here about half of the incoming customers embarked again for St Louis, another two and a half hours flight. At St Louis the rest of the paying passengers left and we were told the plane had been diverted from Oakland to Travis Air Force Base where, as a matter of urgency, it was to be fitted out to collect large numbers of refugees from Saigon. A bus had been provided to take us the one hour's ride to Oakland where Ed collected me and drove me to his home where I was welcomed by his wife Madeline, Aunt Irma and the poodle. After an enormous dinner Madeline asked me if I would like to retire, and as I reckoned I had now been up for some 44 hours, I did just that; but the night was not a long one. At 07.30 next morning Ed banged on my door to say that he was flying down to Los Angeles in Mr Daly's private Convair with a party of business men, and had permission to take me along. The Convair was furnished luxuriously with settees, swiveling chairs and a sky-phone that was used extensively during the flight. A stewardess ensured that the eight or so of us on board did not go hungry or thirsty during the one and a half hour flight. As we flew down at medium height on a cold but clear and sunny day, we followed the coast, Ed pointing out St Simeon, the Hearst domain, overlooking the Pacific Ocean.

The following day Ed took a day off, a rare occasion for him, to show me San Francisco. After visiting Fisherman's Wharf, the Chocolate House, riding on a cable car and driving down the 'crookedest street in the world', we lunched in the rotating restaurant on top of the Fairmont Hotel on Nob Hill - a truly memorable experience. After lunch we drove over the bridge to visit Naomi (Allen) Thomas a British ATA pilot now living in Marin County. We returned via the Golden Gate Park and Chinatown to Oakland where we called in briefly at Jack London Square, and the minute 'pub' with sloping floor and gaslights made famous by the novelist of that name. Next day Ed had arranged for me to stay with Mervin Dunlavy - another ex ATA pilot and his wife, so Ed drove me through the fertile countryside to Calistoga where Mervin - known in the ATA as Alabam - who was also an ex ATA pilot and his wife Carolyn met us and drove me the remaining fifty miles or so to their home on Clear Lake. The weather since I had been in California had been unkind, with blustery winds and rain. Next day we ventured out on to the Lake in a speedboat, but because of a hailstorm we made a speedy return. Alas, I had not prepared myself for this sort of weather in California in April, and consequently spent much of my time in the one set of warm clothes I had brought with me for travelling and returning to the UK. Alabam had planned to show me Nevada so, after a day or two in Lakeport, we set off for Sacremento and the Sierra Nevadas, calling on the way at 'Sams Stage Coast Inn', a saloon which

Ed Heering and ELC at Twyford.

had been restored to its condition in gold rush days, with pianola-type music and an original one-armed bandit. We also stopped at the Nut Tree, a motorway shop and restaurant with its own air-strip, and at the gold rush town of Carson City high in the Sierra Nevadas. We then spent a night at Lake Tahoe where I was introduced to large-scale gambling. Alabam rapidly lost his money at poker and crap whilst I confined myself to putting 10 Cent pieces in a selection of the multitudinous slot machines.

Sadly there was too much snow to permit a visit to Yosemite or even, as we had hoped, to the 'big' trees. The trip ended with a drive back to Ed's through Stockton, where an enormous joint of roast beef awaited us for supper. All too soon the waffles and pancakes came to an end and it was time to return to England. With weather improving I caught a 'stretched' DC8 from Oakland to Chicago. As I was on standby I had to wait to be allowed on a plane to Gatwick, where it was a sunny spring afternoon. Having left a snowy Chicago, several degrees further south, it was impressed on me yet again that English weather is much maligned.

Anyway, thanks to Ed Daly, Ed and Madeline Heering and Marvin and Carolyn Dunlavy, I had enjoyed yet another holiday of a lifetime!

CHAPTER 27

COCHIN

All the time I was in the Civil Service I was paid for sufficient light aircraft flying to keep my licence up, and in 1974 I took time off to train for an instrument rating. For this I started with Thurston at Stapleford Tawney, finishing off with CSE at Oxford. I gained my instrument rating in 1974 but doing no regular flying at the time I found it a far-from-easy challenge. It was however worth it as in May 1976, I was offered a ferry trip in an Islander from the Isle of Wight to Cochin in southern India, something I couldn't have taken on without an instrument rating.

For reasons which we only found out later, two female ferry pilots had been selected for this job because the Islanders, which were for the Indian Navy, would be carrying Indian markings. To reach India the aircraft would have to land at Karachi, Pakistan, a country which, being in dispute with India, was expected to arrest pilots arriving in aircraft with Indian markings. Before departure from England the markings were therefore covered with Fablon on which a British registration was painted. The reason for the females was that, if somehow the Fablon came off en route and the aircraft arrived at Karachi with Indian markings, it was hoped that female pilots would be treated more leniently than males!

The aircraft were due to leave Bembridge on 12th May so, the night before, I took a train and ferry to the Isle of Wight for a night-stop before departing. After a somewhat sleepless night worrying about what I had taken on, I woke to a day of mist and low cloud. Customs, with no regard for flying conditions, said the aircraft would be ready by midday. As I had not as yet flown an Islander Janet Ferguson, a highly experienced ferry pilot who was taking the second aircraft, gave me a twenty-minute low-level circuit for insurance purposes after which, in spite of a continuing forecast of low cloud, we had no option but to take over our aircraft and depart. The aircraft held 'certificates for fitness for flight' valid for only seven days, the time in which, given no delays, we were expected to reach Cochin. What we were to do if we were held up, nobody told us.

Janet and I had agreed on Cannes for our first night-stop. In spite of poor visibility I set off on a VR flight plan crossing the Channel below cloud, but once over France I was forced to climb. We had no transponders but French ATC didn't appear to worry and I did not see the ground again until I had let down over the St. Tropez beacon. From there I followed the coast and after mistakenly making a circuit over Frejus landed at Cannes. The flight had taken me four and a half hours and, as usual, the experienced Janet had arrived before me. We spent the night at an auberge close to the airfield and took off for Naples the next morning in heavy mist. There the refuelling was so slow that it was shortly before sunset by the time we reached Athens.

Here we were told that hotels around the airport were extremely noisy, so we took a taxi into Athens hoping for a good night's sleep; but in Athens all the hotels were full and we had no option but to return to the airport where, in the event, noise in a nearby hotel was not as bad as we had been led to believe. Next morning the airport rang to say that Janet's aircraft had an oil leak and was in Olympic Airways' hangar. Luckily the leak had been found to be from a seal which was repaired reasonably quickly, enabling us to get on our way to our next stop, Larnaca in Cyprus. Near Cyprus we ran into storms and Akrotiri offered us the choice of maintaining altitude and letting down over Larnica, or descending and following the coast. Janet continued to Larnica at 12,000 feet but I descended and followed the coast round the island. Because Beirut was in the process of being evacuated, there was a severe shortage of accommodation at Larnica and all we were offered near the airfield was a very unattractive double room, so we took a taxi to Nicosia, an hour's drive away, where we were lucky to get two rooms in the Kennedy Hotel. Even here, Arabs celebrating their escape laughed, talked and played their radios in neighbouring rooms most of the night!

The dividing line in Cyprus between Turks and Greeks had just been drawn and shopkeepers we talked to the next morning were very unhappy that they could no longer cross to the north side of the island. Our next planned night stop was at Bahrain but, as it was beyond our range, arrangements had been made for us to refuel at Badanah, a landing ground in Saudi Arabia south of the pipeline. This involved

*dian Navy
efender
-BDJW
own by
net Ferguson
om Bembridge
Cochun
2 to 18 May
976.
flew G-BDJZ.*

crossing 10,000 ft mountains to reach Damascus, then turning south to avoid overflying Iraq before picking up the pipeline. We had been warned that if we crossed the Iraq border we could expect to be shot at!

Badanah was a very basic strip staffed entirely by Arabs. Delayed in Cyprus we did not reach there until around 3 o'clock local time and, because an F.27 was expected, an unusual event for Badanah, it was a couple of hours before we were allowed to take off again. This left us insufficient time to make the 500 miles to Bahrain in daylight, but there was no question of improperly dressed females staying the night in a Muslim country so we had no option but to move on. This meant a night landing at Bahrain, my first for many a year.

Next day the relatively short flight to Dubai was followed by a longer one to Karachi. My main memory of Dubai is of the note left by the refueller which read: "Please tight your fuel cap before flying."

The weather for the next part of the route was marginal. Reaching Karachi, I mistakenly set the airfield beacon instead of the outer marker and so found myself overhead the airfield. Tired, with darkness approaching and with no sign of any other aircraft, I made a quick turn and landed on the end of the runway in use instead of continuing to the outer ILS marker – without any complaints or comments from Air Traffic Control. Flying 'against the clock' we had now 'lost' six hours since leaving the UK and, with early starts, were getting seriously short of sleep.

It was after another short night with just four hours sleep and a long walk to our aircraft that we took off for Bombay; this presented certain navigation problems as Flight Plans were not accepted from Pakistan to India. In order to reach Bombay, before turning south aircraft had to continue flying east until out of Pakistan airspace at Bhaunagar, some 350 miles east of Karachi. At Bombay, a flight of just over four hours, we found ourselves very much in 'British' India; everything was done by the book and if you queried the system you were told that this was the way they had been taught to do things. Here the aircraft were given a rigorous inspection by Customs and, by the time they were cleared and refuelled, it was too late to make Cochin which was another five hours or so further on. We had been looking forward to staying at the Horizon Hotel on the beach, but had to settle for the Centaur, a round building with a swimming pool in the centre which was nearer the airfield. Here we each had a double room with bathroom and telephone, luxury indeed compared to recent stopping places. There was also a 24-hour coffee shop. It was the first really comfortable night we had had since leaving England.

We aimed at making an early start but were delayed by servicing inspectors. As radio aids between Bombay and Cochin were few and far between we had decided, unusually, to keep in sight of one another. Unfortunately, once again rules had to be obeyed. Although there were no other aircraft movements, I had to wait three minutes before being cleared for take-off behind Janet and, by the time I got airborne, she was out of sight and I never saw her again! The course took us out to Goa where there was a NDB but after that, for the remaining 600 or so miles, it was a question of following the coast at low level.

I can still visualise the trip. It was a day of blue sky and puffy clouds. On the right, waves over the Indian Ocean signified a monsoon on the way and on the left there were high mountains. We were out of radio contact until within a short distance of Cochin. On the way there I was intrigued to pass a port named Calico Calicut, now Kazhikode. These days few are likely to have heard of it but before WW2, calico was a common name for a plain, unbleached cotton cloth and it was only after I came home that I learnt that this was in fact exported to Europe from there, hence its name.

The Indian Navy station at Cochin was on a grass airfield on Willingdon Island. They were obviously very short of money and facilities were extremely basic. Amongst other things they had no transport. Arrangements had been made for a Britten-Norman representative to meet us and supervise the handover of the Islanders to the Indian Navy; however he had not yet arrived but was expected next day. As Janet was anxious to get back to England I agreed to stay the night and meet him. Having no service transport, a taxi was called to take me to the Malabar Hotel on a point of the Island that jutted out into the harbour.

That evening, accompanied by another hotel resident, I took the ferry to mainland Cochin. It had, we learnt, been the first European settlement in India; it was invaded in 1502 by Vasco de Gama, was next taken over by the Portuguese until in 1795 it fell to the British – who introduced cricket pitches! Next morning while waiting for the Naval Liaison Officer a boat drew up alongside the hotel's front garden with goods to sell and I couldn't resist buying a carved wooden box, inlaid with copper, which I still have. By 09.30 hrs there was still no sign of the Liaison Officer, so I rang the station and shortly afterwards he arrived on a motorbike escorting a taxi which took me back to the squadron office.

As there was still no news of the Britten-Norman representative, I started asking about flights to Bombay. A service from Cochin was run by an Indian Airlines ancient Hawker 748 which, in the prevailing high temperatures, was severely restricted in the number of passengers it could carry. With some difficulty, the Navy managed to book me on a flight due to leave that afternoon. At Bombay I first went to the Air India office to book a flight back to the UK. There was one to Heathrow that left at 02.30 hrs next morning but I was told there was little chance of getting a seat on it; I was therefore happy to book a seat on one leaving at 09 30 hrs next morning, which meant that I could enjoy a night at the Holiday Inn situated on the beach.

So next morning, after an early breakfast, I went down to the beach to wet my feet in the Indian Ocean before taking a taxi back to the airport only to find that the staff, although most apologetic, were unable to say when the plane would leave. The Boeing 747 eventually left about an hour late and was not full, so I got a seat on my own at the back where I could keep my blind up and look out, and sort my papers now stored in my new wooden box. Everyone I had met during my short stay in India had been remarkably good-natured and as efficient as circumstances allowed, leaving me sorry indeed that I could not stay longer to see more of this remarkable continent. The flight in the Islander had taken seven days and just under forty hours flying.

Back in the Adelphi my work continued with the FOI where I remained until I left the CAA in December 1976.

CHAPTER 28

POST CAA – AS A CONTRACTOR

Although I didn't leave the Civil Aviation Authority until the end of December 1976, by October I had already started looking for another job. I approached Engineering and Technical Publications Ltd (ETP), a company based in Wokingham who were advertising for technical authors. As my principal task both at Boscombe and with Fairey's had been report writing, this seemed a job for which I was suitably qualified.

Before anything had been agreed however, I applied in January 1977 for a job with the American firm Digital, who at were based in Reading. I went to see them and they gave me some notes to edit, but I was less than impressed with how they were written; moreover they never paid me either for my visits to them or for any amendments I made, so it all came quickly to an end. In any case I had been in touch again with Brian Goodenough who ran ETP and who supplied technical writers to government contractors. On 28th January I received a letter from him. This offered me a post, as from 14th February, with Hunting Engineering in North Farnborough at a salary of £3,250 per annum, plus £3.55 per day travelling and overtime at £2.43 per hour: this I was happy to accept!

I had been working at North Farnborough for only a few weeks when I mentioned casually during a chat to a colleague in our open-plan office that my eyesight appeared to be not as good as it used to be; to this I received the obvious reply: "Why don't you see someone about it?"

The hut in which we worked was a short distance from the main factory which we had reason to visit from time to time; another short distance beyond this factory were some shops, which included the opticians Leighton's. At an opportune moment and with the excuse of going up to the factory, I went up to the shops and called in at Leighton's. An oculist called me in after a short wait and, after examining my eyes, gave me some notes to take to my GP, saying that I should ring the surgery right away. Puzzled as to what this was all about I nevertheless rang them before getting into my car. On arrival at the surgery I produced my notes, whereupon the lady who was in charge – in the absence of any doctors – immediately rang the Royal Berks Hospital in Reading and told me that I must report there right away – and take a bag!

It appeared I had a detached retina, and the urgency was that if it should drop off there would be nothing that could be done to save my eye. So home I went, packed a bag and went next door to ask my neighbour if she could take me to Reading and although she was entertaining a guest at the time she agreed to do this. As this was before the days of lasers I was in hospital for ten days, and it was another ten days before I returned to work at North Farnborough.

It was soon after this that a vacancy came up with Sperry's in Bracknell who were working on the same classified 'Chevaline' project as Hunting's; this for me would be a much shorter drive, so I asked to be transferred there. At Bracknell I started in the Radiation Section, which carried out radiation tests on various devices. I have few memories of my time in this department except of the visits to the reactors at Harwell and Aldermaston. At Harwell the reactor could not be switched on until their workers there had left at 5 pm, and this late start led to a long day's work and a long drive home on a dark and often wet winter's evening. On the way home we would stop off at a pub in Blewbury, if it was still open, for a late meal.

Later we also took radiation measurements at Aldermaston; here we had to wear shoes with metal toe-caps – which I still have – and film badges which detected radiation. After little more than a year in Radiation I asked to be reclassified as an engineer rather than as a writer and as such, was moved to a less specialist department which dealt, amongst other things, with computerising Chevaline spares. In early 1982 Sperry put the factory (which included Sperry Gyroscope) up for sale; it was taken over by British Aerospace who laid off the contractors, so in March 1982 my going out to work finally came to an end and I was left with much spare time for other interests such as looking after my garden.

In the late 1970s I joined a Concorde Supporters Club - my club number was 151 - and through them I made two flights in Concorde. The first was on 14 November 1978 when I paid £160 pounds for a flight which both took off and landed back at Heathrow. Although

Concorde trip from Nice 7/4/80

during this flight we went supersonic I have few memories of it except that when returning to Heathrow, we landed on the short 23 north-south runway, an unusual one for Concorde. My second flight in Concorde was from Nice to Heathrow, a trip also organised by the Supporters Club. On 7th April 1980, Easter Monday, the Supporters Club offered flights to its members from Heathrow to Nice in a Tristar and to come back in Concorde.

Captain Lawrence was our pilot for the flight in the Tristar, a trip which I also enjoyed. The weather was fine with blue sky all the way apart from some cumulus clouds over the channel. With our relatively small group there was plenty of room in the aircraft and I had a seat by a window from which I watched the sun glinting on a Rolls Royce engine and when we turned, the upward pointing wing. We had a good view of Mont Blanc and the Rhone valley and when descending from our cruising height of 29,000 feet over St Tropez, I looked down on Frejus, Antibes and Cannes before landing over the Promenade des Anglais and a very blue sea at Nice. The flight made me realise that I could enjoy sitting back and being a passenger provided that, as I am an ardent map-reader, I had a window from which I could watch the ground, and my only decision-making was whether to drink gin, whisky or champagne.

We landed at Nice at 13.00 hours and Concorde was not due to take off until 20.00 hours, so there was time to fill in. As it was bank holiday and much else was closed, I decided to take a bus tour which drove us round Nice, Port Villefranche sur Mer, St Jean Cap Ferrat and

Beaulieu sur Mer, stopping off at La Reserve which they told us was one of the Cote d'Azure's famous hotels. By the time we got back to the airport we were within an hour of taking our seats in the Concorde.

The Concorde was G-BOAE or 'Alpha Echo' and the flight number BA9343, our Captain Pat Allen. The flight back in the narrow fuselage with only a pair of side-by-side seats on either side of the gangway was something different, and reminded me of de Havilland aircraft. We were treated with all the luxury of full paying passengers and after the flight we each received the certificate certifying that we had flown in Concorde. Once clear of the west French coast we went supersonic, slowing down as we approached the English coast and as far as I was concerned, it was well worth the £298 I had paid for the pair of flights. My Concorde experience ended on the 10th of September 1996 with a day at Filton in the Concorde flight simulator, another worthwhile experience. I have a number of Concorde souvenirs to remind me of my flights including a jigsaw puzzle of the cockpit, which no doubt in the future years will be equally treasured by one of my numerous nephews and nieces.

CHAPTER 29

RETIREMENT

I had already joined the Wokingham Philatelic Society and now started putting displays in my local stamp shows. Mounting and writing up stamps and making them ready for display called for a considerable amount of time and effort. My first entry to one of the stamp club's shows was in September 1981 when I put an entry into the 'novice' class, winning first prize. By 1984 I had progressed one step up to Club class, where my entry was placed first and in 1985 I entered the Advance class where my entry was again placed first.

I continued entering the Wokingham stamp club's shows but by now was also putting entries into Stampex, the national stamp show which was then held at the Old Horticultural Hall in Westminster. My first entry to Stampex was in 1987 in the National Great British class; this involved preparing four frames of stamps, each consisting of 16 pages, which were then marked for 'Treatment and Importance', 'Knowledge and Research', 'Condition and Rarity' and 'Presentation'. Between 1987 and 1994 I entered Stampex five times, gaining two silver medals and three silver-bronze, the lowest of the medals given. In all classes Gold medals were the top award and to win one of these was to a large extent a question of money, as rare stamps were inevitably expensive as well as hard to come by.

Around this time, with the publication of my book The Forgotten Pilots, a history of the Air Transport Auxiliary, people started asking me to give talks about ATA and its work. For the most part these were to Aircrew Association branches and those of the Royal Aeronautical Society. My first talk in 1976, was to the Manchester Aviation Society, for which John Rabbets very kindly made slides for me from my photographs; I used these at all my talks thereafter. Another of my early talks was given at the request of Danny Boon, Secretary of the Aircrew Association, in a room under Waterloo Station.

One of the most memorable talks was for me, the occasion when Sir Ivor Broom invited me to say a few words at the 50th Anniversary

Pathfinder Force celebrations. These took place over six days in the Cambridge area, ending with a Remembrance Service in Ely Cathedral and a dinner in Cambridge. No dining room could be found in Cambridge large enough to accommodate all those wishing to attend with their wives, so separate dinners had to be arranged; for the men in St. John's College and for their wives in the Garden Hotel. Guest of honour at the ladies' dinner was Baroness Sue Ryder, who had been asked to speak after dinner about her Charitable Foundation. After this Sir Ivor asked me to say a few words about the work of the Air Transport Auxiliary.

Sue Ryder's husband, Leonard Cheshire, had recently died and there was some doubt as to whether she would turn up. She did in fact arrive halfway through dinner. My seat was next to hers and as we had both been at the same school, Benenden, I was able to break the ice when she sat down by recalling people we had both known. This eased a somewhat frosty situation and she later sent me a copy of her book Child of My Love. I met her again at a lunch at the Savoy given by Benenden School to celebrate "Seventy-Five Years of Women's Achievement", at which both Sue and I received awards from the Princess Royal.

My first flight in a balloon was on 18th May 1980. The balloon, G-BCFC, belonged to my friend Dellie Gray-Smith who was a captain in the now defunct airline Dan-Air. This was the first of a number of times when I joined her team, helping generally with taking the balloon out of the trailer, inflating it, then either flying with her in the basket or going with the car to pick the crew up. In the latter case the main part of the job was to find where the balloon had landed. With no mobile phones there was no means, once the balloon was airborne, of communicating with it from the ground, so finding it was a matter of watching its course as best one could. Sometimes it landed somewhere where there was no access for the car, and this could involve knocking up the owner of the property to get access to the balloon in order to pack it up and get it back in the trailer.

For obvious reasons, balloons were only operated in light winds. Flights therefore tended to take place either early in the morning or, more often, at the end of the day when any wind had died down.

Dellie Gray-Fisk's balloon on 18 May 1980.

Outings that come to mind from those days include one in 1981 when we went to a balloon meet at Longleat. The weather on this occasion turned out to be totally unsuitable for ballooning over the whole two days, and ours was never even came out of the trailer. Instead, we drove round the Longleat Safari Park on the first day and on the following day, when all chances of flying had again been given up, we visited the National Trust garden at Stourhead, all of which was enjoyable, but not what we had come to Longleat for!

With no means of steering, balloons depend on the wind for where they go. I remember one occasion when I had been given the job of duty navigator, which involved matching features on ground we were passing over with those on a large-scale map. At this I was being singularly unsuccessful until I realised that the balloon had swung round, and that we were no longer facing in the direction in which we were travelling – a situation with which I was not familiar! Points on the ground which I was expecting to come up did not therefore match up with those shown on my map until I realised that I was no longer looking for them in the right direction! I also remember an occasion late one evening when, anxious to land, Dellie was forced to select a rather small tree-lined field and when coming in to land, brushed lightly through some branches of a tree. This, I commented, was not the way I was accustomed to landing, to which Dellie replied that it shortened the landing run!

In 1983, Joan Hughes and I were amongst a number of other ex-ATA members who attended the 1983 ATA Association's annual dinner at RAF Lyneham. Lord Balfour was one of ATA's guests that year, and Wing Commander Dave Hawkins was the PMC and was also in charge of Lyneham's Hercules training. In the bar after dinner Wing Commander Hawkins asked Joan and I if we would like to come down sometime and try our hands on the Hercules. Naturally we jumped at the idea, but as it was by now the early hours of Saturday morning, we left hopeful but not counting too much on it ever happening.

Three days later Wing Commander Hawkins rang up, inviting us to a dining-in night the following weekend, so on Friday 11th March we presented ourselves at the Officers' Mess at around 2.30 and were shown to rooms in the VIP wing – luxury indeed after the Transit Mess quarters. Three Hercules, it appeared, were about to practise a display to be put on for the coming AOC's inspection and we were to go with them. Joan was to fly with Wing Commander Hawkins, the display leader, and I was to fly with Squadron Leader Mitchell. Full crews were to be carried on the flights including loadmasters, whose job included hanging out of the rear freight doors to direct the pilot as he taxied backwards out of the stand.

The visibility was very poor and after take-off the cloud was so thick that we could only just see the tip of the wing of the aircraft formating alongside us – to the extent that Squadron Leader Mitchell broke off the formation. At 6,000 feet we were in bright sunshine and

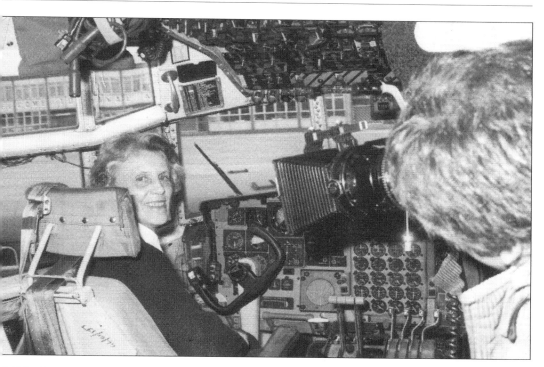

*LC in the
ckpit of a
ercules at
yneham*

formation was resumed. Whilst flying line astern we had a remarkable view of the underside of the leading Hercules. All too soon it was time to return to the murk where in very bad visibility, passes had to be made over a selected spot on the airfield entirely by reference to the ground, in ATA fashion. The RAF were delighted with the poor visibility as it proved that their display could carry on even in bad weather. Disappointing though for Joan and I, but I was at least allowed to make the landing, a most memorable experience. The Hercules, with its landing speed of only some 90 knots, appeared little different to land than types we had flown in ATA.

We got back after around an hour's flight, by which time we needed to change for another excellent dinner and evening at the bar. This time it was after 3 am before we were escorted back to our rooms. If we had been 'royals' we couldn't have been looked after better. We had not only enjoyed ourselves but were extremely flattered at being given the opportunity to fly in the Hercules and to take up so much of their time. A truly memorable 24 hours; thank you once again, Lyneham!

My interest in balloons soon changed to helicopters. It all started with a meeting laid on by the Whirlybirds, the British Women's

Helicopter Association, at Kidlington, Oxford. There, on May 12th 1991, they invited members of the British Women Pilots' Association to join them, and anyone so wishing was offered the chance of a trial lesson in a helicopter. I was one of those who took up the offer and went up in Hughes 300 G-BRTT with CSE instructor Danny Foreman. The flight lasted some 25 minutes and I was of course only allowed 'hands on' when we were in the air. As it always is when flying with an experienced pilot, straight and level flying appeared simpler than I could have imagined and I thoroughly enjoyed the flight. Thus some two months later when some helicopter training started up for the first time at White Waltham with a Robinson 22 two-seater, I booked on regardless of cost for a helicopter private pilot's licence – after all, I was now retired and had time on my hands.

My first lesson was in Robinson R.22 G-NCSH and took place on 22nd July 1991. My instructor was Quentin Smith, whose career since then has been a subject of considerable publicity. The minimum flying hours called for by the Civil Aviation Authority for a PPL (Helicopter) was 40 hours, which had to include ten hours solo. A flying test then had to be taken and examinations passed in Aviation Law, Meteorology, Navigation, Technical (Helicopters) and a recently-introduced one on Human Performance and Limitations – no doubt a standard exam now. There were of course some aspects of these examinations for which, as a fixed-wing pilot, I was already qualified such as air traffic control rules, but the common use of GPS even in light aircraft had by now made considerable changes to navigation.

Getting used to the helicopter controls was a different matter, as they were far more sensitive than those of a fixed-wing light aircraft. Looking back, I find it difficult to believe that I ever achieved a licence! Nevertheless a month or so later, after some seven hours of basic instruction (all entries in my log book were for the first time shown in decimals of an hour) my instructor very bravely sent me off on my first solo. From this I landed somewhat hastily as a result of problems controlling the very sensitive twist-grip throttle which took me a time to get used to. I agree with something I read in a book which said that helicopter flying was "a hands-eyes-and-feet coordination thing". As a fixed-wing pilot the interactive controls of the Robinson certainly took me time to get happy

Celebrating my elicopter licence, October 1992.

with. In another book I read it said that there was a better chance of survival after engine failure in a helicopter than in a fixed-wing aeroplane. This no doubt is true once autorotation and recovery from it has been mastered. In this respect one of the first things I had to learn was that, when simulating engine failure one must not, as in fixed wing aircraft, lower the nose to maintain speed, as under these circumstances rotor speed was the thing that needed watching. One particular test I was less than happy with was that of landing on sloping ground. This was no problem when on smooth rising ground or an otherwise flat surface, but at White Waltham there was no suitable slope. Our instructor had a pile of loose earth built up on the edge of the airfield on which his pupils were expected to practise their 'sloping ground' landings. This involved holding the helicopter at what, for a beginner, was a seriously awkward angle. I was also made to practise vertical climbaways very close to tall trees, which I found worrying!

With the approach of winter my helicopter flying came to a temporary end, as in November I left for New Zealand. There I was given a flight by Hank Courtney in his Jet Ranger from Wellington to Masterton, an ideal way to see a new country from the air. Back home it was not till April the following year that I resumed flying the Robinson. It was now a question of working through the requirements called for by the Civil Aviation Authority before they issued a licence. As this called for only ten hours solo, flights from now on consisted for the most part of flying with my instructor. It was on one of these flights that we saw, for the first and last time in my life, a circular rainbow. I remember reading somewhere the reason for why this occurs but at the time of writing I cannot recall it!

My helicopter licence is dated 8th October 1992. I took my test with Mike Smith, Quentin's father, a very experienced helicopter pilot. For this he came down to White Waltham, and when the test had been completed we hover-taxied across the airfield back to the 'black' hangar where the helicopter was kept. White Waltham produces a good crop of mushrooms most years and, half way across the airfield, Mike spotted some and I was asked to hover while he leant out of his door to pick them! A fitting end to a somewhat gruelling day.

I have a sister, brother-in-law, a niece and family living in Southrepps, Norfolk, south of Cromer. By car this is a good three-to-four hour drive so when I drive up there I usually stay the night. Each year in summer I used to fly up for lunch, taking a friend for company, and we would land at Southrepps airfield which was within a couple of miles of the house. I have particular memories of our first visit in 1988; it was with Peter Clifford in a Piper Cherokee hired from the West London Aero Club at White Waltham. Although I knew exactly where to look for the airfield we had some difficulty in finding it. It had only one short grass runway—on that day downhill – with tall crops growing alongside it. We couldn't find a windsock and the only obvious building was an old beach hut. After a couple of circuits we decided that this was indeed an airfield and I told Peter, a Piper agent and very experienced pilot, that he had better do the landing – which in the event called for quite a bit of braking!

I have to say that now the airfield is well organised, but I remember my sister telling me a short time after our visit that it was being enlarged to take helicopters! Anyway, we were collected by the family and after a splendid lobster lunch returned to White Waltham. But back to the helicopter story.

Having got my helicopter licence, I thought: "Why not fly up to Southrepps in the Robinson and make a weekend of it?" So I asked

Quentin, who was then unmarried, if he would like to come as once there he would be able to give anyone so wishing a trial flight. Quentin jumped at the idea, so on the 17th October we took off in Robinson G-BTVU for Southrepps. By now the route by road and by air was familiar to me and we flew over the house before reaching the airfield. Here, instead of continuing to the airfield, Quentin suggested landing on the tennis court – something I would certainly not have undertaken on my own. The family came out to meet us and, after lunch, whilst I stayed talking to them, Quentin offered to give joyrides to anyone interested; an opportunity which several accepted. When he came back we were amazed to see the helicopter in the drive, within feet of the house, and there it remained for the rest of our stay. Before returning south we needed to refuel and for this a small bowser was brought from the airfield up the road. Taking off from the drive, which had quite a few trees around, called for a seriously vertical climb-out which of course was undertaken by Quentin. Once safely in the air I resumed the flying and we flew back to White Waltham; the end of a particularly memorable weekend.

22 G-BTVU side uthrepps Hall, rfolk.

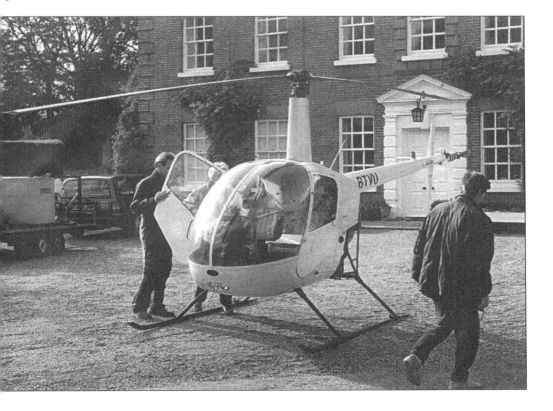

In September 1993 Quentin was replaced as Sloane's helicopter instructor at White Waltham by Peter Driver. I continued to keep up my flying, mostly by making short cross-countries, but occasionally flying for a change with Driver and once or twice with Georgina Hunter-Jones. By the spring of 1995 I realised that I was not doing enough to improve, or even keep up, my helicopter flying. Fitting in suitable weather with helicopter availability meant devoting virtually ones whole time to keeping an eye open as to whether a flight could be arranged. Fixed wing aircraft were more readily available for hiring and for me, called for less concentration especially when taking off and landing than the helicopter, in which serious attention had to be given to virtually all aspects of flight. Was it, I asked myself, really worth devoting any more time – and money – to keeping up my flying licences? I decided that the time had come to give more time to my house, my garden, my writing and the many aviation societies of which I was a member. I therefore decided, as far as flying was concerned, to call it a day.

Snapshots

L-R:
ELC,
Jennie Broad,
drey Sale-Barker,
Gabby Patterson,
Pauline Gower
Hatfield 1940.

Jack Death
TA Operations
fficer at White
Valtham, hands
an Hughes her
rk for the day.

Pauline Gower
with King
George VI and
ueen Elizabeth;
White Waltham
February 1942.

In the cockpit of a Liberator

Climbing aboard a Spitfire

Hugh Field, GAPAN Master, invests ELC with livery, 1980.

The Duke of Kent meets women pilots at White Waltham. Front left-right; Margot Gore, Joan Hughes, ELC, Monique Agazarian. September 1991.

With Battle of Britain pilots, L-R W/Cdr 'Paddy' Barthropp, ELC, A/Cdr Peter Brothers. Spitfire Society presentation to Jeffrey Quill, 12 December 1991.

Moth Club meeting at Woburn 1998.
Basil Lockwood-Goose,
ELC,
John Cunningham.

Reunion with a Spitfire.
The late Matin Sargeant with ELC.
2000.

Joan Hughes and ELC with Caroline Grace (centre) a modern day Spitfire pilot. September 1991.

AIR TRANSPORT AUXILIARY

CERTIFICATE OF SERVICE

To *Flight Captain Eleanor Lettice Curtis*

This Certificate has been issued by way of Record and in recognition of your Services with the Air Transport Auxiliary.

The A.T.A. was formed in 1939 upon the Declaration of War by Great Britain, for the purpose of delivering His Majesty's Aircraft to the Royal Air Force and the Royal Navy, and for Air Transport tasks auxiliary to the War Effort.

You have played your Part and shared in the Achievements of an Organisation which has every Reason to be proud of its Record.

COMMODORE,
COMMANDING OFFICER, A.T.A.

SELECTED INDEX